MODERN BRITISH HISTORY ★ A Garland Series

Edited by
PETER STANSKY and
LESLIE HUME

THE CRISIS OF THE OLD POOR LAW IN ENGLAND 1795–1834 ★ An Interpretive Essay

Peter Dunkley

Garland Publishing, Inc.
New York & London ★ 1982

Library of Congress Cataloging in Publication Data

Dunkley, Peter, 1943–
The crisis of the old Poor Law in England, 1795–1834.

(Modern British history ; 11)
Bibliography: p.
Includes index.
1. Poor laws—Great Britain—History. I. Title.
II. Series.
KD3299.D86 1982 344.42′0325 81-48357
ISBN 0-8240-5153-X 344.204325

All volumes in this series are printed on acid-free,
250-year-life paper.
Printed in the United States of America

For my Mother and Father

TABLE OF CONTENTS

Preface

The last two decades have seen growing interest in the transformation of British government in the nineteenth century.[1] Of particular concern has been the advent of centralized inspectorates, which were established for the purpose of more closely and effectively enforcing social legislation. One of the first casualties of this heightened interest was an older interpretation that saw the first half of the century as an era when the functions of government were reduced to a minimum in accordance with a prevailing laissez-faire ideology.[2] Students of the period are now generally agreed that government was then, in fact, both growing and actively re-defining its responsibilities and operations. If these developments did not constitute the immediate origins of the British Welfare State, at least it is here that we may identify the emergence of certain elements that have come to be characteristic of twentieth-century forms of government.[3] Beyond this point all agreement ends. What is sometimes called "the nineteenth-century revolution in government" has been the source of a major, continuing debate on the nature of administrative development and the ways in which social policy was formulated and implemented.[4]

---

[1] An interim report on work in the field may be found in R.M. MacLeod, "Statesmen Undisguised," American Historical Review, LXXVIII, 5 (1973), 1386-1405.

[2] The classic statement is A.V. Dicey, Lectures on the Relation Between Law and Public Opinion in England During the Nineteenth Century (London, 1905).

[3] See D. Roberts, Victorian Origins of the British Welfare State (New Haven, 1960).

[4] The most important contributions are O. MacDonagh, "The Nineteenth-Century Revolution in Government: A Reappraisal," Historical Journal, I, 1 (1958), 52-67; D. Roberts, "Jeremy Bentham and the Victorian Administrative State," Victorian Studies, II (1959), 193-210; H. Parris, "The Nineteenth-Century Revolution in Government:

Although this clash of divergent views has undoubtedly helped to shed light on significant aspects of nineteenth-century government, until recently the debate suffered from a preoccupation with the details of day-to-day administration and the "internal" affairs of the bureaucracy in its various guises. When the essay that follows was first written (1975), the study of social policy was largely a branch of administrative history, and the extension of government activity was often explained as an autonomous process.[5] Even critics of the latter view couched their objections in ways that attributed government growth to the influence of abstract, a priori ideas and the efforts of a handful of social reformers, "statesmen in disguise." To be sure, in some cases perspectives of this sort may be appropriate; I have myself used these same terms of reference to examine an obscure government agency in the 1820s and 1830s.[6] Nevertheless, it seems equally clear that there are limits to the usefulness of such an approach. The elaboration of social policy and the reorganization of administration were necessarily the work of individuals, but ultimately the wider society impinged upon the process, since, in the largest sense, government was (and is) concerned with matters of authority and function in society. Any analysis that ignores or slights this dimension will fail to recognize sufficiently the interaction between social change and the transformation of government.

In the last few years, attention has increasingly turned to the social implications of administrative

---

A Reappraisal Reappraised," Historical Journal, III, 1 (1960), 17-37; J. Hart, "Nineteenth-Century Social Reform: A Tory Interpretation of History," Past and Present, 31 (1965), 39-61.

5 A slightly modified version of Chapter III subsequently appeared as "Paternalism, the Magistracy and Poor Relief in England, 1795-1834," International Review of Social History, XXIV, 3 (1979), 371-97.

6 "Emigration and the State, 1803-1842: The Nineteenth-Century Revolution in Government Reconsidered," Historical Journal, XXIII, 2 (1980), 353-80.

development.[7] Conscious efforts have been made to integrate more fully social and administrative history in order to avoid what is seen as an incomplete definition of government and its purposes.[8] In the opinion of Paul Richards, for instance, state and society are too often separated in the work of those who are steeped in the niceties of bureaucratic proliferation and the play of systematized ideas.[9] As valuable as this criticism is, it must also be admitted that the social perspective, too, carries with it certain pitfalls, especially if claims for its insights are not carefully guarded. The transformation of government cannot be regarded as a mere reflection of social change and the disruptions and conflicts left in its train. The formulation of social policy, a matter of fundamental concern in modern times, only began at the point when "intolerable" conditions were identified.[10] The ways in which policy-makers perceived the problems confronting them, the means they had available to them, the effectiveness of those who remained attached to traditional institutions, and the influence of special interests affected the timing and, above all, the shape of official response. It is the proper and essential role of social history in all of this to explain the context in which problems were discerned, means were devised, effectiveness was assessed, and influence was realized.

The reform of the poor laws in 1834, which resulted in the creation of the most celebrated central inspector-

---

7 See, e.g., A.P. Donajgrodzki, ed., Social Control in Nineteenth Century Britain (Totowa, N.J., 1977).

8 A good example is R. Johnson, "Educational Policy and Social Control in Early Victorian England," Past and Present, 49 (1970), 96-119.

9 "The State and Early Industrial Capitalism: The Case of the Handloom Weavers," Past and Present, 83 (1979), pp. 91-92.

10 A. Briggs, "The History of Changing Approaches to Social Welfare," in E.W. Martin, ed., Comparative Development in Social Welfare (London, 1972), pp. 10-11.

ate of the nineteenth century, seems particularly suited to contextual interpretation. For reasons that will become clear later on, the poor relief system and the difficulties and controversies it gave rise to in the four decades before its reform constituted a major problem for government. In order to appreciate this adequately, it is necessary to look behind the deliberations of select committees and royal commissions, beyond the debates in Parliament and the Cabinet, to the social relationships which gave the poor law problem its urgency and which finally required some sort of comprehensive treatment. Seen from this angle, the policy-making process encompassed far more than a coming together of the ideas of individual reformers and the views of isolated politicians in London. At issue were vital questions of discipline and order in that contemporary attitudes to poverty were conditioned by the need to regulate and control the forces of social change. This, perhaps more than anything else, composed the context in which decisions were made and investigations were conducted.

The following essay is designed to consider poor law reform from this specific point of view. No attempt is made to offer a general survey of the concerns and events that led to and shaped reform. Still less does the argument insist that the factors examined here represent the only meaning of reform or that reform can be "reduced" to a monocausal explanation, however broad in scope. Rather the purpose is to show ways in which the New Poor Law of 1834 may be seen, in part, as a reaction to the breakdown of social cohesion in the English countryside; this should then reveal some of the intricate connections between social dysfunction and government decision-making in the period. The picture presented is one of worried politicians groping for some means of ensuring social stability without impeding further agricultural development or endangering the interests of landed property. This serves as the basis for what is hopefully a useful perspective on the changing attitudes of England's rulers toward the poor and the problem of poverty in rural society.

* * *

It gives me great pleasure to be able to take this opportunity to thank formally those who gave me a helping hand at various stages in the preparation of this essay. Anyone who has worked in the principal English archives will already be aware of the high standards of organization and skill which invariably characterize their operation. The staffs of the Round Room at the Public Record Office, the Manuscript Room at the British Library (formerly the British Museum), the Watson Library at University College, London, the John Rylands Library, Manchester, the Reading Room of the Department of Paleography, Durham, the Goldsmith Library at the University of London, and the Bodleian Library, Oxford, all provided the measure of expertise and attentiveness that makes the historian's job easier and more enjoyable. I remember with particular gratitude the kindness of the director of the Royal Archives, Mr. Mackworth-Brown, who allowed me access to the Melbourne Papers, and the patience and friendliness of Her Majesty's archivists in the Round Tower at Windsor.

Another kind of assistance came from the two institutions in which I have thus far spent the greater part of my academic life. The Center for Research in International Studies and the trustees of the James Birdsall Weter Fellowship at Stanford University provided the financial aid upon which a graduate student is necessarily dependent, and for this I am most grateful. I should also like to thank the President and Directors of Georgetown University, who made available funds for the preparation of a single-spaced typescript.

My greatest debts are to a number of individuals upon whom I have relied for all manner of support. Leslie Hume offered me encouragement when I needed it most. My old friends Pete and Barbara Thompson were, as usual, unstinting in their hospitality and companionship when I stayed with them while doing research in Durham. Professor Paul Seaver made some valuable comments on an early draft and, more importantly, taught me the joys of Tudor-Stuart history. A very special thanks must go to my undergraduate advisor and graduate supervisor, Professor Peter Stansky. In my experience he is without peer in his capacity and will to create a humane and stimulating environment in which to learn and work. His many devoted students will appreciate that I am not alone in this view.

In thanking my wife, I find it impossible to list her contributions. My debt is so large that only she can truly know how much I owe her.

Washington, D.C.
April 1981

I. Introduction

The poor relief system of the early-nineteenth century represented a governmental function of unusual scope for the period. Relief expenditure in 1818 nearly equalled the expenditure of all the civil departments of the national government combined.[1] When seen in conjunction with the way in which England was actually governed, this bald fact takes on added importance. Up to about 1833, the compass of central administration was largely confined, both in conception and fact, to the collection of revenue, the defense of the realm, and the preservation of internal order.[2] This resulted in local government shouldering the main burden of governing the country, while at this level, the amount of time, attention, and money devoted to poor law matters exceeded all other concerns put together.[3] Consequently, county, divisional, and parochial administration remained for most people the most conspicuous form of government activity throughout our period, and the operation of the poor laws was that part of it which touched most often the daily lives of ordinary Englishmen.[4]

Any alteration in such a system was bound to cause some comment, but contemporaries were especially aware of the significance of the Poor Law Amendment

---

1 Sidney and Beatrice Webb, *English Poor Law History: The Last Hundred Years* (Hamden, Conn., 1963), Pt. II, Vol. I, p. 2.

2 David Roberts, *Victorian Origins of the British Welfare State* (New Haven, 1960), p. 13; Henry Parris, *Constitutional Bureaucracy* (London, 1969), p. 22.

3 W.E. Tate, *The Parish Chest* (Cambridge, 1960), p. 188.

4 A.P. Thornton, *The Habit of Authority. Paternalism in British History* (Toronto, 1966), p. 79; J.H. Clapham, *An Economic History of Modern Britain: The Early Railway Age, 1820-1850* (Cambridge, 1926), p. 351.

Act, the so-called New Poor Law, which received the king's assent in August 1834. Sir Robert Peel, leader of the opposition and later twice Prime Minister, called it "a great experiment," and Edwin Chadwick, a member of the Royal Commission of Inquiry appointed to prepare the measure, never tired of portraying the act as "one of the most important administrative improvements of our times."[5] William IV declared the New Poor Law to be "one of the greatest measures that has ever passed the legislature."[6] The members of the Whig cabinet that adopted and introduced the bill believed that the act was one of the prime accomplishments of their distinguished administration, and that it would insure their reputation in posterity.[7] Even so august a statesman as William Gladstone remained convinced at the end of a long career that the passage of the measure rendered "high honour" to the Whig administration of 1830-34.[8]

The wide-ranging provisions of the amendment act in themselves justify its recognition as a milestone in social legislation. In providing for the central direction of poor relief administration, the measure established three poor law commissioners at Somerset House in London, who in turn were to rely on assistant

---

5 Parliamentary Debates [hereafter cited as Hansard], 3rd series, XXXVI, 1088; memo by Chadwick, August 1846, Box #20, Chadwick Papers (University College, London).

6 Quoted in Roberts, Victorian Origins of the British Welfare State, p. 303.

7 Lord Lansdowne/Lord Grey, n.d., endorsed: 9 July 1834, Box 38/10, and Lord Holland/Lord Grey, 28 August 1834, Box 34/4, Grey Papers (University of Durham); Lord Howick/Lord Melbourne, 12 April 1836, Box 7/51, Melbourne Papers (Royal Archives, Windsor); memo by Lord John Russell, c. November 1837, P.R.O. 30/22/2F, fos. 202-03, Russell Papers (Public Record Office, London).

8 Autobiographical note of 6 September 1897. Quoted in John Morley, The Life of William Ewart Gladstone (London, 1903), I, p. 115.

commissioners in the provinces to enforce their directives and oversee all relief activities. More permanent, standardized, and professional modes of administration were to replace the hodge-podge of administrative practices in England's multitudinous parishes in an effort to eliminate the amateurism and corruption of parochial authorities. The commissioners were empowered to form unions of parishes, which were then to be placed **under the direction of boards of guardians made up of elected local ratepayers, with county magistrates sitting as ex-officio members. Directly responsible to these** boards was to be a local cadre of salaried officials, which included relieving officers, workhouse masters and matrons, union clerks, rate collectors, and medical officers, with ultimate control over the length and terms of their employment in the hands of Somerset House. Finally, the commissioners were expected to ensure national uniformity in the distribution of aid by the implementation of relief principles enumerated in the 1834 report of the Royal Commission of Inquiry of 1832-34.[9]

The tendency of recent work, including my own, has been to question the practical effect of this legislation on the actual distribution of aid at the local level.[10] However, the fact remains that at the time of

---

9 Report from His Majesty's Commissioners for Inquiring into the Administration and Practical Operation of the Poor Laws (London, 1834). A very useful reprint of this seminal document has recently appeared in the Pelican Classics series; edited by S.G. and E.O.A. Checkland, this edition will be the one used in this study. References below will be to P.L.C. Report of 1834, Pelican edn.

10 See my "The 'Hungry Forties' and the New Poor Law: A Case Study," Historical Journal, XVII, 2 (1974), pp. 329-46; Norman McCord, "The Implementation of the 1834 Poor Law Amendment Act on Tyneside," International Review of Social History, XIV, 1 (1969), pp. 90-108; M.E. Rose, "The Allowance System Under the New Poor Law," Economic History Review, Second Series, XIX, 3 (1966), pp. 607-20.

its passage the amendment act promised to engender fundamental change in the administration of poor relief. Regardless of occasional pious statements that the measure would merely reinforce traditional relief practices, a national bureaucratic authority was to be given the prerogatives of revamping an ancient system of local government and regulating poor relief without the need to procure local consent or parliamentary ratification.[11] In effect, Parliament showed itself ready to abdicate its powers of directing the largest single branch of civil administration in the country (based on annual expenditure), and in its own place to substitute an independent central authority whose latitude in the formulation of policy was theoretically hampered only by a tenuous responsibility to the current ministry. Although the implications of these proposals were not always adequately understood,[12] the New Poor Law remains an impressive indication of the determination among the politicians at Westminster to relegate to others the responsibility of their class for the operation of one of the major institutions of their society.

The effect of the act on the duties of the large landowners in the local administration of relief reinforces this point. As we shall see, the landlords in their capacity as justices had a special concern with and control over the distribution of aid in the pre-reform system, the Old Poor Law.[13] After 1834, however, the power of the magistracy perceptibly diminished. By including the justices as ex-officio members of the boards of guardians, the New Poor Law opened the elected positions to non-members of the bench. Since there was no appeal against the decisions

---

[11] See Webb, English Poor Law History: The Last Hundred Years, Pt. II, Vol. I, p. 81.

[12] See, e.g., Hansard, 3rd series, XXIII (17 April 1834), 897.

[13] See Chapter III.

of a board of guardians, save to the poor law commissioners at Somerset House, the magistrates in effect now shared with others of lesser rank what had previously been their role as ultimate arbiters in local relief matters. There was often (but certainly not always) no incompatibility of interests between the traditional ruling group and their colleagues on the boards, but unless the justices showed unstinting diligence in board affairs, the control of local relief policy could easily pass to guardians of more moderate social standing. This was always a very real possibility, for it seems that the attendance of the magistrates trailed off substantially after the act had been established in the local communities.

In those parts of the country where no major landowner predominated or took an interest in relief affairs, the landed interest was most vulnerable to the innovations of the New Poor Law. Without a strong lead from a concerned and powerful magnate in protecting the integrity of the area of the landlords' personal influence, the assistant commissioners were free to form poor law unions according to topography and the general distribution of population. In such instances, it was not uncommon for agricultural parishes to be united with those in populous rural centers and medium-sized urban areas. In the more "unruly" agrarian counties, where large landed proprietors were relatively scarce, such as Cambridgeshire, Essex, Cumberland, Middlesex, Buckinghamshire, Oxfordshire, Somersetshire, and Herefordshire, the ratepayers were in a position to assume control of the boards. These developments -- the loss of agricultural parishes to population centers and ratepayer-controlled boards -- weakened the hold of the landowners over local administration, for the smaller gentry, in their capacity as magistrates, had often been able to dominate both types of rural constituencies under the Old Poor Law.[14]

---

[14] For all of the above, see my "The Landed Interest and the New Poor Law: A Critical Note," English Historical Review, LXXXVIII, 349 (1973), pp. 836-41. This interpretation is controversial. See Anthony

The relief policy that the New Poor Law envisaged is also indicative of the readiness of the politicians at Westminster to encourage sweeping change in an institution that was notorious for its heterogeneity and the ad hoc, personal administrative practices of those charged with its operation. The amendment act itself principally provided for the machinery from which policy decisions would emanate and through which they would be carried out at the local level, but it was generally assumed that policy would be devised in conformity with the views of the Royal Commission of Inquiry. At the heart of the commission's recommendations regarding relief policy was a belief in the efficacy of self-help in promoting the moral regeneration of the laboring poor. The main object to be kept in view, therefore, was to ensure that the poor would be reluctant to look to the public authorities for aid. This could be accomplished, the commissioners maintained, through the general implementation of an all-encompassing, universally-applicable principle: "The first and most essential of all conditions [they established] . . . is that [the pauper's] situation on the whole shall not be made really or apparently so eligible as the situation of the independent labourer of the lowest class."[15] That is to say, industry and thrift, the hallmarks of independent labor, would spring from a policy that systematically rendered the condition of the pauper less appealing than that of the employed laborer. Just as important, such a principle would, for the first time, establish a standard definition of need. Only those who were prepared to accept aid under mandated terms would come within the purview of public relief authorities.

These overarching concerns established certain requirements pertaining to the instruments of relief

---

Brundage, "The Landed Interest and the New Poor Law: A Reappraisal of the Revolution in Government," ibid., LXXXVII, 342 (1972), pp. 27-48; and idem, "The Landed Interest and the New Poor Law: A Reply," ibid., XC, 355 (1975), pp. 347-51.

[15] P.L.C. Report of 1834, Pelican edn., p. 335.

dispensation. The commissioners recognized that to produce a climate of "less eligibility" the administration of relief would have to be highly controlled. Following the lead of apparently successful experiments in scattered parishes in Nottinghamshire and other parts of the country, the commission fixed upon the workhouse as the most effective method in implementing a policy of less eligibility.[16] Within the confines of such an establishment, relief of the laboring poor could be carried out with an exactitude that would be impossible if relief were to be continued out of doors, regardless of the conditions under which it was distributed. The commission's first and most important recommendation, therefore, was that "all relief whatever to able-bodied persons or to their families, otherwise than in well-regulated workhouses . . . shall be declared unlawful. . . ."[17] In this way the offer of relief under the prescribed circumstances could be used as a genuine "test" of the need of the applicant for aid.

Although the universal claims of these doctrines were unprecedented in the search for a solution to the pauper problem, in some respects the commissioners' views were consistent with those of previous poor law investigators. Perhaps the most distinctive feature of the commissioners' deliberations was the degree to which questions of rural poverty occupied their attention, the agrarian south being an area of prime concern.[18] There was nothing new in this. Because of regional disparities in the distribution of indigence,[19] contemporaries had long conceived pauperism to be almost exclusively a rural problem.[20] As late as the 1820s,

---

16 See J.D. Marshall, "The Nottinghamshire Reformers and Their Contribution to the New Poor Law," Economic History Review, Second Series, XIII, 3 (1961), pp. 382-96.

17 P.L.C. Report of 1834, Pelican edn., p. 375.

18 Brian Inglis, Poverty and the Industrial Revolution (London, 1971), pp. 337-38.

19 Infra, pp. 35-38.

20 M.E. Rose, The Relief of Poverty, 1834-1914

the national debate on pauperism assumed England to be a rural society to an extent that was no longer true, the special issues of urban poverty receiving little or no serious examination in the pre-reform period.[21] Like the royal commission of 1832-34, select committees appointed to investigate the poor laws in 1817, 1824, 1828, and 1833 confined their chief observations to the rural districts of the southern counties.[22]

An obsessive concern with able-bodied pauperism further narrowed the discussion of the poor law problem. Even though the able-bodied poor and their dependents -- as opposed to the impotent poor (the aged, infirm, and orphaned) -- made up only one part of the pauper host, the royal commission declared aid to the able-bodied to be the "master evil" of the relief system, while claiming that "the allowances to the aged and infirm are moderate."[23] The practical consequences of this

---

(London, 1972), p. 12; and idem, "The Allowance System Under the New Poor Law," p. 614.

21 Norman McCord, "Aspects of the Relief of Poverty in Early 19th-Century England," in R.M. Hartwell, ed., The Long Debate on Poverty (Old Woking, Surrey, 1972), p. 96; J.R. Poynter, Society and Pauperism: English Ideas on Poor Relief, 1795-1834 (London, 1969), p. 22.

22 Report [from the Select Committee] on the Poor Laws, P[arliamentary] P[apers], 1817, VI, p. 16; Report [from the Select Committee] on Labourers' Wages, P.P., 1824, VI, p. 5; Report [from the Select Committee] on [That Part of the Poor Laws Relating to] the Employment or Relief of Able-Bodied Persons [from the Poor Rate], P.P., 1828, IV, p. 8; Report [from the Select Committee] on Agriculture, P.P., 1833, V, p. vii; P.L.C. Report of 1834, Pelican edn., pp. 152-53.

23 P.L.C. Report of 1834, Pelican edn., p. 114; Rose, "The Allowance System Under the New Poor Law," p. 607; Webb, English Poor Law History: The Last Hundred Years, Pt. II, Vol. I, p. 89. S.E. Finer estimates that in 1832, the able-bodied constituted from one-third to one-half of the poor receiving aid. The Life and Times of Sir Edwin Chadwick (London, 1952), p. 81.

conclusion are evident in the record of the commission's proceedings: in a report of more than 450 pages (in the Pelican edition), consideration of relief to the impotent poor is confined to ten pages. Again, the commissioners were in conformity with the general drift of contemporary opinion on the poor laws. The first major investigation of the relief system following the Napoleonic Wars had propagated a similar view: "The casualties . . . of sickness and old age, do not constitute the greater proportion of the demands upon the poors rate which have raised it to its present high amount; a much greater proportion . . . consists of the allowances distributed in most parts of England to the labouring poor. . . ."[24] Even before the appointment of the royal commission, Nassau Senior, one of its most influential members, had reached the same conclusion. In a published letter to Lord Howick in 1831, he proclaimed that "the relief of the able-bodied, is itself the grand abuse of the English Poor Laws -- the source from which all their other abuses have flowed."[25] It is not entirely surprising, therefore, that the commission's recommendations should have been directed to only one aspect of the poor law problem, regardless of pretensions concerning their general applicability.

Still, one is immediately struck by the commission's failure to come to grips with the sources of poverty in English society. No account was taken of the fluctuations of trade in the creation of unemployment, of the effect of the introduction of machinery into a manual labor market, of the differing structural problems of agricultural and industrial economies, or of the individual circumstances that produce able-bodied destitution. Consequently, the commissioners presented a lopsided view of English pauperism, lopsided because they had confined their attention to the south (which suffered from difficulties peculiar to an agricultural

---

24 Report on the Poor Laws, 1817, p. 13.

25 N.W. Senior, A Letter to Lord Howick on a Legal Provision for the Irish Poor (London, 1831), p. 43.

economy), to able-bodied pauperism (which probably accounted for no more than one-half of the poor receiving relief), and to the narrow remedy of the twin principles of less eligibility and the workhouse test (which were founded on an assumption of the prevalence of voluntary pauperism). Yet despite this, the commissioners' report remained the most authoritative and influential document of its kind in the nineteenth century, Lord Brougham in 1834 calling it "a mass of evidence the largest, the most comprehensive, the most important and the most interesting that perhaps was ever collected upon any subject."[26] Not only did the Whigs accept its findings and recommendations; they relied almost exclusively upon it for justification of the far-reaching change in relief administration that they proposed.[27]

How is this to be explained? It is certainly not sufficient to attribute the influence of the ideas enshrined in the commissioners' report simply to the force and logic of their arguments. To do so would be to confer on those arguments a power of their own, independent of the pressures and considerations that had prompted the appointment of the royal commission in the first place. More importantly, to consider "the principles of 1834" in isolation would be to ignore the fact that social legislation such as the New Poor Law formed part of the wider response of England's rulers to dislocation in a society undergoing substantial change. The eighteenth century saw the landed interest at the pinnacle of its power, dominating with only few exceptions the political, administrative, judicial, religious, and military institutions of the country. While the nation's economy had attained a complexity that included important commercial, and even manufacturing, interests, the chief economic sector continued mainly to center on the landed estate, from which the governing elite drew their income and social prestige,

---

26 Hansard, 3rd series, XXV (21 July 1834), 224.

27 Ibid., 3rd series, XXIII (17 April 1834), 877.

and which formed the basis of their control of what was still essentially a rural world. The world of the early-twentieth century, in contrast, had become notably industrial and urban, its institutions in the hands of a diversity of classes that looked to a broad field of economic and social activities as the source of status and authority. Even the workers had to a large extent become organized and articulate and were on the verge of sustained and independent political action. The threat to social order during a transformation of such magnitude is obvious; even the most optimistic social progressives recognized the hazards. As Harriet Martineau told Lord Howick in 1844, "the greatest comfort . . . is in the splendid promise for the future, if the pressing danger [of discontent] can be averted. A population so vast & energetic, [growing] up in a new consciousness of needs & rights, moral, political & physical, opens a whole field for future statesmen, if order can but be kept through the transition process."[28]

In the first part of the nineteenth century, the erosion of local rural communities and the breakdown of communal consensus and cohesion were central elements in this "transition process." In these conditions, the maintenance of order demanded a whole range of adjustments and adaptations on the part of those who governed England. Before new approaches to government could be fashioned, however, it was often first necessary for the rulers to recognize that the old techniques of social discipline and control were no longer useful, that their main function was no longer being fulfilled. This was particularly so in the case of poor law reform, for the poor laws had been bound up with the problem of social stability since their inception in the sixteenth century.[29] As a result, the large landowners had a special interest in their operation, an interest that was recog-

---

[28] H. Martineau/Lord Howick, 19 January 1844, Box 114/14, Grey Papers.

[29] J.D. Marshall, The Old Poor Law, 1795-1834 (London, 1968), p. 10; M.E. Rose, ed., The English Poor Law, 1780-1930 (Newton Abbot, Devon, 1971), p. 11.

nized in the prominent place accorded the magistracy in the administrative hierarchy of the relief system. A study of the actions of the landed magnates in this capacity and of their shifting attitudes to personal involvement in a traditional system of popular patronage should, therefore, help to elucidate the aristocratic response to change and disorder in early-nineteenth-century rural life. Only when this is done will it be possible to begin to explain the influence and success of the Royal Commission of Inquiry in 1834.

II. Order and the Poor Law Problem

In the early-nineteenth century, the large owners of agricultural property remained at the center of power and authority in England.[1] From this group were drawn the local leaders of rural society and the predominant portion of the political leaders of the entire nation. Although this dual role gave strength to the rule of the landed interest, it could also be a source of tension whenever the priorities of the political leaders at Westminster differed from those of their colleagues engaged in the daily routine of governing the local communities. For the most part, however, a series of institutions that helped to bind the landed interest together and to define it as a ruling elite mitigated distinctions between what George Kitson Clark has called the "provincial" and the "political" aristocracies.[2] Among these insitutions was the Commission of

---

[1] Various means might be used to identify this elite. In this regard, F.M.L. Thompson points to the size of landed estates as an important criterion. The lesser gentry are said to have held estates of from 1,000 to 3,000 acres, while the greater gentry were those with estates of from 3,000 to 10,000 acres. Ranging above the greater gentry were the owners of the great estates, the true landed aristocracy, whose number included more than just the titled nobility. David Spring has also named 1,000 acres as being the lower limit of the proper landed estate. F.M.L. Thompson, *English Landed Society in the Nineteenth Century* (London, 1963), p. 112; D. Spring, *The English Landed Estate in the Nineteenth Century: Its Administration* (Baltimore, 1963), p. 1.

[2] G. Kitson Clark, "The Repeal of the Corn Laws and the Politics of the Forties," *Economic History Review*, Second Series, IV, 1 (1951), p. 5. In order to avoid confusion, it should be noted that the terms "provincial aristocracy" and "political aristocracy" are used in this essay in Kitson Clark's sense as comprising the entire landed interest rather than merely its upper reaches.

the Peace, which comprehended the greater part of the major landowners in England.

This magistracy constituted the most essential component in the machinery for the enforcement of law at the local level. The importance of the justices of the peace in this regard was not founded solely on the social and economic influence that the large proprietors enjoyed in rural society. Rather, it followed in some part from the wholly inadequate institutional arrangements for the maintenance of order in this period. The magistrates were armed with a savage criminal code, which was sometimes used for the purpose of doling out exemplary punishment to selected defendants at major trials.[3] Yet the heavy sentencing that at times came in the wake of popular disturbances merely underscores the poverty of local resources for implementing the law against wholesale "insubordination." As Lord Melbourne, the Home Secretary in the Whig government of 1830-34, told one of his correspondents, "many evils arise not so much from the inadequacy of the law as from the difficulty of enforcing it. . . ."[4] This was a concern even more apparent to those who had the task of administering the law in the provinces.[5]

The enforcement problem had its principal source in the archaic provisions for a local constabulary. The court leet of the manor or the parish vestry had the authority to designate a parish constable, but they often failed to take this precaution. Even in those cases where an officer was actually appointed, he was too often unsuited for his duties; as the substantial and industrious farmers avoided this onerous service,

---

[3] A.J. Peacock, "Village Radicalism in East Anglia, 1800-50," in J.P.D. Dunbabin, Rural Discontent in Nineteenth-Century Britain (London, 1974), pp. 48-49.

[4] Lord Melbourne/Lord Derby, 11 January 1831, in Lloyd C. Sanders, ed., Lord Melbourne's Papers (New York, reprint edn., 1971), p. 122.

[5] Sir George Crewe/Lord John Russell, 28 March 1836, P.R.O. 30/22/2A, fos. 352-53, Russell Papers.

the position fell into the hands of the illiterate and indolent in many parishes.[6] The difficulties arising from such a situation were reflected in increasing pressure to create "a Proper & Efficient Constabulary Force in the Rural Districts."[7] After the Captain Swing disturbances of 1830-31 and the poor law riots of 1834-35 had revealed once again the inability of the authorities to disperse tumultuous assemblies, the government was made keenly aware of the need to establish more reliable instruments for law enforcement at the local level. The Duke of Richmond informed Melbourne at the end of 1835 that "every days experience proves to me more and more that we must have a more efficient system of Rural Police . . . I wish you & John [Russell] would take the subject into your consideration, for I am convinced of the paramount necessity of something being done."[8]

Attempts were in fact made to put the office of parish constable on a more permanent and professional footing. The constable act of 1830 (11 Geo. IV, c. 47) empowered vestries to appoint paid officers, but this had little effect. In Worcestershire, for example, not one rural parish had a salaried constable by 1843, and in one magisterial division of the county (Pershore), the bench had only been able to induce one parish even to consider the matter.[9] In 1839 Parliament passed a more ambitious scheme for the establishment of

---

[6] David Williams, The Rebecca Riots: A Study in Agrarian Discontent (Cardiff, 1955), pp. 56-57.

[7] Sir George Crewe/Lord John Russell, 28 March 1836, P.R.O. 30/22/2A, fos. 352-53, Russell Papers.

[8] Duke of Richmond/Lord Melbourne, 23 December 1835, P.R.O. 30/22/1E, Russell Papers. **The poor law riots also provided other would-be reformers of the law enforcement** system with yet another instance to prod ministers into taking action. Edwin Chadwick/Lord John Russell, 29 September 1836, P.R.O. 30/22/2C, fo. 179, Russell Papers.

[9] Gen. Thomas Marriott/Pershore Union Guardians, 10 March 1843, Box #3, Chadwick Papers.

a local police, which permitted counties to raise a constabulary force. But again this did not prove sufficient for the country's needs. As late as 1856, about half of the counties had not implemented the act, and in some of the remainder, provisions had been made for the policing of only part of their areas.[10]

These ramshackle arrangements dictated that in any extraordinary circumstances, extraordinary measures would have to be resorted to in order to preserve the peace. This often necessitated the magistrates' swearing in special constables from the general population as a supplement to the tiny company of regular constables. Being composed of undisciplined civilians, however, a special constabulary could not always be relied upon to counter successfully large assemblies.[11] During the Otmoor disturbances of 1831, for instance, an Oxfordshire magistrate complained to the Home Office that the special constables sworn to protect the moor from anti-enclosure mobs were "perfectly inefficient."[12] The use of special constables also had an added disadvantage in that they were subject to divided political loyalties; this could become alarmingly apparent at times of high political excitement. After popular disorders had become characteristic of the movement for parliamentary reform, the government found that even men of property were not always ready to aid in the suppression of riot. In October 1831, Lord Melbourne told the Prime Minister, Lord Grey, that "there undoubtedly prevails a much greater indisposition to be

---

[10] Parris, Constitutional Bureaucracy, pp. 230-31. Because the acts of 1830 and 1839 were permissive, ratepayer resistance on the grounds of expense often stood in the way of those who wished to set up an effective police force. Ibid., pp. 230-31; Williams, The Rebecca Riots, pp. 59-60.

[11] Nicholas C. Edsall, The Anti-Poor Law Movement (New Jersey, 1971), p. 102.

[12] Quoted in Bernard Reaney, The Class Struggle in 19th Century Oxfordshire. History Workshop Pamphlets, No. 3, (Oxford, n.d.), p. 47.

sworn in Special Constables & to assist in the protection of property, than at this time last year. This arises from the prevalence of party spirits & the violent . . . animosities engendered by the [parliamentary] elections."[13] Two days later Melbourne wrote to the Lord Chancellor in a similar vein: "We shall have the whole Country in a blase [sic], & we have not the same means of putting it out, as we had last year . . . personal animosities have been engendered by these elections, [and so] hardly anybody will lend a hand to save his neighbours property . . . The difficulty of inducing Persons to be sworn in Special Constables is ten times as great as it was last year."[14] Matters were rendered even more desperate when, as in the case of the Rebecca riots in Wales in the early 1840s, the rioters themselves were of the same class from which the justices normally recruited the special constables.[15] It is clear that when men refused to serve as special constables or neglected to discharge their duties when sworn, the very foundations of social order were endangered.

When the challenge to local authorities was sufficiently menacing, they might turn to the yeomanry, or militia, for aid in restoring order. Indeed, this force had been one of the chief bulwarks of social stability in the eighteenth century.[16] But after the Napoleonic Wars, the yeomanry were permitted to atrophy in strength and training. While the available cavalry force numbered about 18,000 in 1817, it had dropped to approximately 14,000 by 1838; this left some counties, such as Lancashire, Durham, and those in South Wales,

---

13 Lord Melbourne/Lord Grey, 29 October 1831, Box 41/2, Grey Papers.

14 Lord Melbourne/Lord Brougham, 31 October 1831, Brougham Papers (University College, London). See also Lord Melbourne/William IV, 28 December 1831 (copy), Melbourne Papers.

15 See Sir James Graham/Sir Robert Peel, 4 September 1843, Add. MSS. 40449, fos. 19-20, Peel Papers (British Library, London).

16 Max Beloff, Public Order and Popular Disturbances, 1660-1714 (Oxford, 1938), p. 149.

practically denuded of yeomanry corps.[17] The force had deteriorated to such an extent by the early 1840s that the disturbances of those years caught the authorities dangerously short-handed, so much so in fact that the Peel government was obliged to consider increasing the number of corps.[18] Still, the obstacles to employing the yeomanry went beyond the problem of falling strength. A yeomanry force was expensive to maintain, especially in those instances when disturbances were protracted, which necessitated paying large numbers of irregular troops for long periods of time. In the 1830s the Whig government felt these financial considerations so strongly that they were moved to reduce further the number of men liable for call-up.[19] In addition, there was, as with the special constables, the question of the reliability of those groups that provided the necessary manpower. During the Swing riots of 1830-31, for example, the landed proprietors of Kent and Sussex were unable to induce the farmers to form themselves into a corps without first promising to reduce rents and tithes.[20] An even more important deterrent to the use of yeomanry to quell unrest was growing fears that it exacerbated discord by inflaming the passions of the populace, the members of the yeomanry themselves often being parties to the conflict and the force having generally an unsavory reputation for brute repression.[21]

---

17 F.C. Mather, Public Order in the Age of the Chartists (Manchester, 1959), pp. 143-45.

18 Sir Robert Peel/Duke of Wellington, 24 August 1842, Add. MSS. 40459, fos. 294-95, Peel Papers; Sir James Graham/Lord Francis Egerton, 4 September 1842 (copy), MS. Film 113/53A, Graham Papers (Bodleian Library, Oxford).

19 Lord John Russell/Lord Howick, 11 January 1838, Box 122/1, Grey Papers.

20 J.L. and Barbara Hammond, The Village Labourer, 1760-1832 (London, 1912), p. 255.

21 Mather, Public Order in the Age of the Chartists, pp. 146-47.

In short, the yeomanry shared all the defects that were evident in ill-trained, ad hoc local bodies constituted to supplement an inadequately organized regular police force. In complaining of the suspected disloyalty of the Dorsetshire yeomanry in 1831, Melbourne pointed out the most pronounced shortcomings of such bodies:

> We must not conceal from ourselves [he told Sir Herbert Taylor, the king's private secretary] that the real weakness and inherent vice of all institutions of this nature, from a regiment of volunteers down to a posse of special constables, is that, being taken immediately from the body of the people, and not having habits of military obedience, they are in times of strong popular feeling either divided within themselves by discordant opinions, or so possessed and heated with the prevailing popular sentiment, that either they cannot be depended upon for acting at all, or are entirely incapable of conducting themselves with that steadiness, coolness, and impartiality which are so absolutely required in such circumstances.[22]

It is no wonder, then, that the government did not encourage the too frequent or prolonged employment of the yeomanry in the suppression of disorder.

Although the regular troops at the disposal of the government in times of exceptional civil discord were not subject to similar objections, here too there were definite checks to their utilization. The primary apprehension was that the available troops would prove insufficient to handle widespread or concerted up-

---

22 Lord Melbourne/Sir Herbert Taylor, 25 October 1831, in Sanders, ed., Lord Melbourne's Papers, pp. 134-35.

heavals.[23] "It is impossible," Sir James Graham lamented during the northern disturbances of 1842, "even if you had a standing Army ten times greater than the British, to provide Troops for every town and village throughout the manufacturing districts. . . ."[24] This factor severely restricted the deployment of troops, for contingency measures often demanded that the military remain in uneffected areas at times of unrest in other parts of the country. This may be seen most clearly in the government's response to the Chartist rising in Wales in 1839. Lord Normanby, then the Home Secretary, outlined for Lord Melbourne the restraints he faced in providing competent troops to support the local authorities: "I did not think the 45th a very good Regt to send [to Wales] . . . but the alternative would have been 'the Rifles' from [Weedon?] and to remove them would have left the Birmingham Country and the Midland Towns unprotected and I therefore thought it best to leave that Regt lest the example [of the Welsh rising] should be followed in other districts."[25]

These kinds of fears sprang from a recognition of the deficiencies of large-scale military operations as a method of coping with civil discord. The effectiveness of the army resided in its ability to apply concentrated, overwhelming force at critical points; to disperse it was to nullify its most advantageous feature. Its practical use was therefore confined to the immediate area within which it was stationed, which perforce left large parts of disturbed districts without adequate protection. As Graham complained to Sir Robert Peel in 1842, "even a slight disturbance, simultaneous at distant points, creates a want of

---

23 See, e.g., Hansard, 3rd series, I, 634.

24 Sir James Graham/H.J. Parker, 24 August 1842 (copy), MS. Film 113/52B, Graham Papers. See also Lord Melbourne/Lord John Russell, 6 November 1839, Box 14/79, Melbourne Papers.

25 Lord Normanby/Lord Melbourne, 5 November 1839, Box 10/82, Melbourne Papers.

military Force. . . ."[26] During rural riots in 1831, the anti-poor law disturbances in East Anglia in 1835, and again in the Rebecca riots of the 1840s, rioters carefully avoided head-on confrontations with trained troops, which for a time rendered military force largely ineffective as a means of coping with disorder.[27] Hence, in order to thoroughly crush regional outbreaks, particularly those of considerable geographical extent, it was necessary that the government make heavy military commitments. It is somewhat startling to discover, for instance, that the 12,000 troops sent to the Midlands in 1812 to contain the Luddite rebellion greatly outnumbered the army that had accompanied Wellington to the Peninsula only four years earlier.[28]

It should be noted that in this discussion of law enforcement problems, most of the examples cited have been drawn from the 1830s and 1840s. Even after the creation of the Metropolitan police force in 1829, the government had available to it only limited resources in the event of provincial upheavals. Besides being extremely unpopular outside London, the number of Metropolitan police was small, and they could only be spared for short periods of time.[29] Until well into the nineteenth century, consequently, the Home Office -- the department of central government with special responsibility for internal security -- remained anxious to avoid any intervention in civil disorder for as long as possible.[30] Given this situation, it is not surpris-

---

[26] Sir James Graham/Sir Robert Peel, 24 July 1842, Add. MSS. 40447, fo. 53, Peel Papers.

[27] Reaney, The Class Struggle in 19th Century Oxfordshire, p. 50; Edsall, The Anti-Poor Law Movement, p. 36; Williams, The Rebecca Riots, pp. 225-26.

[28] E.J. Hobsbawm, "The Machine Breakers," in idem, Labouring Men (London, 1964), p. 6.

[29] Edsall, The Anti-Poor Law Movement, p. 103.

[30] R.R. Nelson, The Home Office, 1782-1801 (Durham, N.C., 1969), pp. 159-60; Mather, Public Order in the Age of the Chartists, p. 75; Edsall, The Anti-Poor Law Movement, p. 103; Williams, The Rebecca Riots, pp. 192-93.

ing that ad hoc local means for dealing with chronic unrest continued to be the first and most significant line of defense against "servile" challenges to the rule of property and the law.

With this knowledge of the haphazard institutional provisions for law enforcement we may now appreciate more fully the difficulties of the magistracy in governing the local communities. The vulnerability of the bench, especially in rural districts where sufficient forces were most lacking, may be detected in the propensity of magistrates to make concessions when confronted with unruly bodies of men.[31] In the eighteenth century, it was not at all uncommon for justices to yield to the demands of food rioters by fixing the price of grain or by conducting or sanctioning forced sales at below current market prices.[32] This tradition was carried into the nineteenth century when rural disorders in East Anglia in 1816 at first met with magisterial agreements to raise wages and increase poor relief dispensation.[33] Even when disturbances were serious enough to involve the central government in their suppression, such as the Captain Swing riots of 1830-31, the initial reaction of provincial authorities was to submit to the impositions of the rioters.[34] In the case of Swing, landlords reduced rents in order that wages might be raised and condoned the destruction of threshing machines; although the wage concessions were short-

---

[31] F.O. Darvall, Popular Disturbances and Public Order in Regency England (London, 1934), p. 238.

[32] R.B. Rose, "Eighteenth Century Price Riots and Public Policy in England," International Review of Social History, VI (1961), p. 288; E.M. Hampson, The Treatment of Poverty in Cambridgeshire, 1597-1834 (Cambridge, 1934), p. 192.

[33] A.J. Peacock, Bread or Blood. A Study of the Agrarian Riots in East Anglia in 1816 (London, 1965), pp. 80-81, 102.

[34] Dunbabin, Rural Discontent in Nineteenth-Century Britain, p. 299; Hammond, The Village Labourer, p. 256.

lived, the hated machines did not stage a comeback for several decades.[35]

Critics of the justices, particularly those among the political leaders, usually attributed such behavior to timidity or incompetency. Panic among the magistrates and their almost inevitable requests for troops at the first hint of disorder lent credence to these charges.[36] One of Robert Peel's abiding problems while he was at the Home Office in the 1820s was in persuading the justices to shoulder the burden of putting down sporadic outbreaks of discontent without looking to the government for assistance.[37] Lord Melbourne, too, on assuming the secretaryship from Peel in 1830, felt the need to stiffen the magistrates' backbones by issuing sternly-worded circulars on what was expected of them in the way of handling rural disturbances.[38] Even the king expressed his disgust with the justices for their failure to execute the law against troublemakers and for "the urgent manner in which the Magistrates and Country Gentlemen apply on all occasions for the Aid of the Military or Constabulary Force."[39]

There were undoubtedly some valid grounds for these censures of an unpaid magistracy that was largely appointed without regard for ability to perform in crisis situations. Even so, critics were not entirely

---

35 J.P.D. Dunbabin, "The 'Revolt of the Field': The Agricultural Labourers' Movement in the 1870s," Past and Present, 26 (1963), pp. 89-90; E.J. Hobsbawm and George Rudé, Captain Swing (New York, 1968), pp. 234-35; Introduction by R. Samuel, in Reaney, The Class Struggle in 19th Century Oxfordshire, pp. i-ii; Hobsbawm, "The Machine Breakers," p. 17.

36 J.T. Ward, The Factory Movement (London, 1962), p. 196; Mather, Public Order in the Age of the Chartists, p. 141; Williams, The Rebecca Riots, p. 56.

37 Norman Gash, Mr. Secretary Peel (London, 1961), pp. 344-61.

38 Hobsbawm and Rudé, Captain Swing, pp. 234-35.

39 William IV/Lord Melbourne, 12 April 1831, Melbourne Papers.

fair in attributing the reluctance of provincial leaders to become personally involved in the repression of disobedience to simple fear of reprisals. To regard the magistrates as mere executors of a body of statute law was, and is, to ignore the restraints of custom and popular values that informed their actions as community leaders. In examining the sources of disruption in the life of rural communities, we come face-to-face with a culture that could accord a certain legitimacy to at least some types of disorder.[40] In the eighteenth century, this was likely to take the form of local rulers encouraging or ignoring attacks on religious dissenters, profiteering grain dealers, or organizers of domestic industries.[41] In the early-nineteenth century, after it had become more objectionable to countenance insubordination in the lower orders, the survival of this tradition may be seen in some of the magistrates' active sympathy for the Swing rioters and the popular protests against the introduction of the New Poor Law.[42] Even in those instances where there was an absence of tender feeling towards unruliness, the authorities generally expected, at least in the initial stages of conflict, to assume roles as mediators.[43] This enjoined an emphasis on "moral suasion" rather than

---

[40] J.D. Chambers, Nottinghamshire in the Eighteenth Century. A Study of Life and Labour Under the Squirearchy (New York, 1966), p. 49.

[41] Ibid., p. 216; E.P. Thompson, "The Moral Economy of the English Crowd in the Eighteenth Century," Past and Present, 50 (1971), p. 95; Beloff, Public Order and Popular Disturbances, p. 70; Rose, "Eighteenth Century Price Riots and Public Policy in England," p. 291; Hobsbawm, "The Machine Breakers," p. 16.

[42] Hobsbawm and Rudé, Captain Swing, p. 257; J.D. Chambers and G.E. Mingay, The Agricultural Revolution, 1750-1880 (New York, 1966), p. 145; Edsall, The Anti-Poor Law Movement, p. 101.

[43] E.P. Thompson, "Patrician Society, Plebian Culture," Journal of Social History, VII, 4 (1974), pp. 395, 403.

physical confrontation and accounts in part for the unwillingness of some magistrates to take the lead in the organization of defense associations or the command of a system of police.[44]

The readiness of authority to make certain concessions to the threat of disorder suggests that social stability encompassed far more than the effectiveness of coercive mechanisms. This might be expected in a paternal society, where benevolent concern for the humble supplements punishment in the interests of social harmony. Paternalism alone, however, is not sufficient to characterize what E.J. Hobsbawm calls "the relational complex" that was most distinctive of English country life in the early-nineteenth century.[45] Such a concept too narrowly focuses attention on the rulers of society, defining social relations in terms of their actions and attitudes. Perhaps a more useful concept may be found in subordination, for subordination conditioned a wide range of social interaction and was especially relevant to relations between the propertied and the poor. This in turn requires an examination of deference in that deference, above all, rationalizes and sanctions subordination. By deference is meant the individual commitment to or acceptance of a moral order that legitimizes "the individual's own political, material, and social subordination."[46] This clearly affords the crucial link in the kind of social hierarchy that typified English society in our period.[47] That is, a structure of stratification presupposes claims of superiority and the general acceptance of those claims, since the structure could not exist in the face of massive

---

[44] Darvall, Popular Disturbances and Public Order in Regency England, p. 235.

[45] "From Social History to the History of Society," Daedalus, C (1971), pp. 31-32.

[46] Colin Bell and Howard Newby, "The Sources of Variation in Agricultural Workers' Images of Society," The Sociological Review, XXI, 2 (1973), p. 233.

[47] Edward Shils, "Deference," in J.A. Jackson, ed., Social Stratification (Cambridge, 1968), p. 130.

assertions of equality.[48] The strength of such a social order is therefore to be found in its minimization of personal interests, for each individual is subsumed in the broader determinant of established social gradations.[49] It is obvious, then, that if deference were prevalent enough, the existing order need not fear occasional aspirants for a larger share in the benefits accruing to that order.

For this reason, subordination and the hierarchy of ranks resting upon it were conceived to be the fountainhead of social cohesion in the eighteenth century.[50] What Max Weber called "traditional legitimacy" gave practical force to these concepts in rural life, as custom and the collective memory of the community, rather than formal rules or coercion, sanctioned subordination to recognized authority.[51] The appeal to tradition, however, carried with it a need to maintain the personal connections that for centuries had been at the heart of social relations in the countryside. Although deference and its concomitant, status, might be accorded to persons at a distance, it is essentially a relationship of face-to-face personal interaction, which necessarily limits the range of its direct and strongest influence.[52] Edward Shils puts it this way: "Deference systems tend to become territorially dispersed into local systems which are more differentiated

---

48 D.E.G. Plowman, W.E. Minchinton, and Margaret Stacey, "Local Social Status in England and Wales," The Sociological Review, X, 2 (1962), p. 164.

49 See Gertrude Himmelfarb, "The Writing of Social History: Recent Studies in Nineteenth-Century England," Journal of British Studies, XI, 1 (1971), pp. 162-63.

50 A.W. Coats, "The Classical Economists and the Labourer," in E.L. Jones and G.E. Mingay, eds., Land, Labour and Population in the Industrial Revolution (New York, 1968), p. 106.

51 Plowman, Minchinton, and Stacey, "Local Social Status in England and Wales," p. 167.

52 Ibid., p. 164.

to those who participate in them than is the national system."[53] This does not imply a conflict between those in the "local systems" and the leaders or institutions of the wider society, as persons in local associations (such as early-nineteenth-century English rural communities) are linked to the impersonal, universalistic national society by means of what might be called patronage.[54]

It must be stressed that the personal element is uppermost in a patron-client relationship, personal obligation taking precedence over individual interests. This should be a warning against adopting a too narrow definition of deference. Deference often comes to be conceived as a series of duties that a subordinate owes to his superior when in fact the deference relationship assumes a good deal of reciprocity.[55] In no sense does deference imply an abandonment of self-respect on the part of inferiors, for their relationship with those above them is seen as one of "partnership" rather than servitude.[56] This ideal of mutuality and interdependence points to an organic conception of society that is incompatible with the degradation of subordinates. A patron, too, has obligations that are instrumental in sanctioning and perpetuating the attachment and loyalty of his clients.[57]

The English gentry of the early-nineteenth century, as will become clear, often accepted such responsibilities as a part of their function and saw in them additional justification for the power and prestige they enjoyed as large landowners.[58] It is

---

53 Shils, "Deference," p. 126.

54 Bell and Newby, "The Sources of Variation in Agricultural Workers' Images of Society," pp. 233-34.

55 Ewing Goffman, Interaction Ritual (Chicago, 1967), p. 59.

56 H. Newby, "The Deferential Dialectic," Comparative Studies in Society and History, XVII, 2 (1975), p. 145.

57 Thornton, The Habit of Authority, pp. 71-72.

58 Eugene C. Black, ed., Victorian Culture and Society (New York, 1974), pp. 267-68.

in this respect that some recent discussions of the political behavior of the time have been somewhat misleading, for they have neglected to emphasize sufficiently the interchange implicit in deferential relationships.[59] A more satisfactory view of the dynamics of deference is found in contemporary conceptions of the obligations of each component of the social order. Nathaniel Kent's remarks of 1796 may be taken as the articulation of an ideal guide for social relations in rural society: "In the prosperity of agriculture, there are three persons who have a natural tye [sic] upon each other: the gentleman of landed interest -- the farmer -- and the labourer. Their degrees of interest are different, but their connexion must be permanent, as they cannot subsist without the aid of each other. Protection is due from the first -- humanity from the second -- and obedience from the third."[60] It is noteworthy that Kent's observations assume the three-tier economic structure that had already established itself in English agriculture by the early-eighteenth century. Yet social function, rather than economic or political role, primarily differentiates each interest within the community. What may be termed the deference ideal, or model, ensures stability and respect for rank by insisting upon the obedience of the laboring poor, but at the same time it makes the cohesiveness, or "connexion," of the social structure dependent upon the operation of reciprocal obligations.

All this is not to say that early-nineteenth century rural England exhibited the signs of an ideally deferential society, for this was manifestly not so. Poaching, cattle-maiming, and rick-burning were as much a part of the rural scene as the forelock-tugging laborer and his curtseying daughter. Nevertheless, the

---

[59] D.C. Moore has gone so far as to argue that political contacts between the landowners and their clients were "clearly one-sided." See "The Other Face of Reform," Victorian Studies, V, 1 (1961), p. 16.

[60] Quoted in Hobsbawm and Rudé, Captain Swing, pp. 47-48.

significance of all such models is that they provide a norm to which actual activity can from time to time be referred.[61] This places a premium on the image of those who aspire to be the recipients of deference, as "deference - entitlement" often requires the attribution of "goodness" to assure a complete and continuing reconciliation to subordination and obedience.[62] This has obvious significance for stability in a society noted for great disparities in wealth and privilege.[63]

Such concerns were not lost on England's provincial rulers in the early-nineteenth century. The mark of a wise landlord was bestowed on those who cultivated feelings of gratitude among their subordinates, while a dissolute proprietor could be expected to disregard his responsibilities to those who depended on his goodwill for their livelihood.[64] Particular importance was attached to a landlord's conformity with local custom, which might include expectations of uneconomic behavior in the setting of rents, the lavish support of local organizations and festivals, the maintenance of a large and bountiful household, and so forth.[65] Among the most important elements in reconciling the poor to the superordination of the landlords was the manner in which they executed their role as the agents of justice. Certainly decisions of the bench were considered to have an effect on the standing of the magistrates in the eyes of the community; as the High Constable of Newbury remarked, "a Magistrate does not like to make himself unpopular or obtain the reputation of being severe . . ."[66] The desire of individual justices to main-

---

[61] Goffman, Interaction Ritual, p. 60.

[62] Shils, "Deference," pp. 105-06.

[63] Bell and Newby, "The Sources of Variation in Agricultural Workers' Images of Society," p. 244.

[64] H. Thrope, "The Lord and the Landscape," in Dennis R. Mills, ed., English Rural Communities: The Impact of a Specialised Economy (London, 1973), p. 31.

[65] Peter Laslett, The World We Have Lost (New York, 1965), p. 76.

[66] "First draft of evidence on Rural Police," c. 1837, Box #3, Chadwick Papers.

tain a name in the community for fair-dealing could, of course, have an influence on the bench's attitude to local disorder. Even Melbourne abhorred the ferocity of magisterial repression in the manufacturing districts at the same time he execrated the leniency of the bench in dealing with rural disturbances.[67]

The primacy of personal authority in the deference model dictated that the magistracy should actually be seen to be just. In this respect the gentry were fortunate in being a rentier class, for this effectively removed them from the direct exploitation of the laboring poor; their tenantry, trade, or taxation undertook this task for them.[68] A certain social utility may thus be seen in the moral order that a Dr. Edwards posited in 1783: "Gentlemen have no right to be farmers; and their entering upon agriculture to follow it as a business is perhaps a breach of their moral duty."[69] In contrast, the gentry enjoyed the high visibility of their role as magistrates, through which they might cut a figure by granting appeals for poor relief, acceding to applications for mercy, or taking action against profiteering grain merchants, forestallers, and greedy millers. This, of course, necessitated the gentry's physical presence on the bench or on occasions of similar communal rituals, which partly explains why the social duty of the landlord to be in residence in the country became well-nigh axiomatic.[70] In discussing the responsibilities of the bench, Eardley Wilmot, like so many others, stressed the need for the individual magis-

---

[67] Lord Melbourne/Lord John Russell, 1 December 1838, Box 13/102, Melbourne Papers. Even in industrial areas the magistracy was mostly comprised of the local landed gentry. Edsall, The Anti-Poor Law Movement, p. 104.

[68] Thompson, "Patrician Society, Plebian Culture," pp. 388-89.

[69] Quoted in Lord Ernle, English Farming Past and Present (Chicago, 1961), p. 207.

[70] E.W. Bovill, English Country Life, 1780-1830 (London, 1963), pp. 66-68.

trates to become personally identified as the chief source of popular patronage: "The most important of their duties [is] their residence in the various places in the county where they [live], and where they [are] enabled to act as friends of the poor, and heal disputes as arbitrators and referees."[71]

These comments echo those of Nathaniel Kent in seeing the magistracy's most suitable image to be that of protectors of the poor. Even at the national level, policy was sometimes couched in terms that assumed a need to bind more closely the poor's welfare to the affairs of the rich. In 1843, a select committee of the House of Commons, for instance, recommended the extended use of garden allotments because it had "a peculiarly good effect upon the relations between the landowner and his cottage tenants; increasing his acquaintance and interest in their circumstances, and exciting in them more thankfulness and respect."[72] The last phrase of this statement gives some hint of the motivations of self-interest many times evident in paternalistic behavior.[73] Unquestionably the local rulers expected "thankfulness and respect" in return for their investment in popular patronage.[74] On the other hand, reliance on such a means of social control involved the governors in various commitments to their subordinates. The paternalist traditions of the authorities might add to or take their direction from local custom, which necessarily called forth popular anticipations of proper conduct and ob-

---

71 Quoted in C.H.E. Zangerl, "The Social Composition of the County Magistracy in England and Wales, 1831-1887," Journal of British Studies, XI, 1 (1971), p. 116.

72 Report [from the Select Committee] on Labouring Poor, (Allotments of Land), P.P., 1843, VII, p. v.

73 See G.E. Mingay, English Landed Society in the Eighteenth Century (London, 1963), pp. 186-87.

74 See, e.g., testimony of T.L. Hodges, M.P. and J.P. of Kent, in Minutes of [Evidence Taken Before] the Select Committee of the House of Lords [Appointed to Consider] of the Poor Laws, P.P. (Lords), (19. of 1830-1), CCLXXXVII, p. 16.

servances on the part of the authorities. To the extent that this was the case, the rulers were in some measure the captives of the communal culture.[75] This, of course, does not mean that as a class they were particularly notable for their restraint in disciplining the poor or utilizing the instruments of repression to combat insubordination. All the same, if the proprietors hoped to retain their credibility as the poor's protectors and thus ensure obedience, there was one obligation which the authorities could not avoid, that of making certain that the laborers had at least a bare subsistence.[76] As a consequence, sundry *ad hoc* measures were designed to hedge round the laborers' livelihood, each varying greatly in effectiveness and range of use. These might include the occasional implementation of the traditional legislation against the internal grain trade, the hiring of redundant labor for make-work schemes, the resistance of landlords to the introduction of labor-saving machinery, visitations of the proprietors' female relatives to the sick poor, the subsidization of benefit clubs, and most important of all, the careful administration of the poor laws.[77]

The prominence of these imperatives in rural life arose from, and contributed to, a tradition that saw -- and I am paraphrasing Nathaniel Kent here -- the subsistence and well-being of the entire community to be dependent upon the social connections between the different degrees of interest within the agricultural economy.[78] By the early-nineteenth century, some

---

75 Thompson, "The Moral Economy of the English Crowd in the Eighteenth Century," pp. 78-79.

76 A.W. Coats, "Economic Thought and Poor Law Policy in the Eighteenth Century," *Economic History Review*, Second Series, XIII, 1 (1960), p. 43.

77 E.L. Jones, "The Agricultural Labour Market in England, 1793-1872," *Economic History Review*, Second Series, XVII, 2 (1964), pp. 330, 333.

78 *Supra*, p.28. Dunbabin, *Rural Discontent in Nineteenth-Century Britain*, p. 13.

conservative social commentators were observing that the economic individualism of a rising urban and industrial society threatened to undermine the social accountability of each component of the social order; this presaged the disintegration of society because the "chain of connexion" between the rich and the poor would thereby be broken.[79] The implication was that the intrusion of self-interest, economic or otherwise, endangered a structure of interdependency and mutual respect and concern between social ranks. Melbourne's advice to a correspondent on how to handle the advent of trade unions among agricultural workers in Dorsetshire shows the practical application of such sensibilities:

> I shall be very glad to learn that the farmers refuse to employ those labourers who have engaged in the union, and I am of opinion that it will be much better that they should do so of their own accord, and from themselves, than upon the recommendation of the magistrates. . . it will have a greater effect upon the labourers themselves, and will be less offensive to them than it would be if it could be attributed, as it would be, solely to the influence and interference of the higher classes of society. At the same time the farmers should receive every encouragement and support in such proceedings, always taking it for granted that they have themselves acted justly, and have not generally attempted to reduce the wages of the labourers below their fair and natural level.[80]

---

79 Asa Briggs, "The Language of 'Class' in Early Nineteenth-Century England," in Asa Briggs and John Saville, eds., Essays in Labour History (London, 1967), pp. 45-46.

80 Lord Melbourne/James Frampton, 31 March 1834, in Sanders, ed., Lord Melbourne's Papers, pp. 157-58.

The Home Secretary, a man not known for tenderness in dealing with insubordination, is concerned here with the appropriate response to the violation of a social order founded on the need to minimize (and conceal) the play of naked economic interest. Trade combinations are seen as a breach of that order because they are grounded on a class interest which seeks to alter the "fair and natural" wages of a paternalistic society. The paternal responsibilities of "the higher classes of society," however, hamper retaliatory action, as is revealed in Melbourne's main concern to protect the image of the landlords as the friends of the poor. The farmers might be expected to impose sanctions against the workers so long as they remain within local norms on wage levels, but the proprietors' own economic stake in the outcome of the conflict would give particular offense to the community if they were to become too obviously involved. This would compromise deference and thereby endanger the social hierarchy.

It must be understood that the rise of trade unions among the agricultural laborers is itself an indication of the breakup of a society of interdependency and mutuality between ranks, if in fact such a society had ever existed. Throughout the period of this study, profound socio-economic changes were occurring within the rural communities that threatened to undermine obedience and cause social instability. At bottom, the problem concerned the increasing difficulty of the agricultural laborers to procure subsistence. The growth of rural population after the mid-eighteenth century contributed substantially to a crisis of poverty in many parts of the country. It is true that during our period the cultivated area of the land was expanding and agricultural output was rising, but this was not always accompanied by a corresponding increase in the use of labor resources. Methods such as the more efficient organization of estates, the application of new fertilizers, and the use of improved farm implements in areas lacking a sufficient labor force accounted for a large part of the increased production.[81] Hence, a major factor in the spread of poverty was not population growth per se, but the inability of the rural economy to absorb it, which, coupled with the disinclination of agricultural laborers to migrate, created serious concentrations of surplus labor and pressures on wages.[82] The effects of these developments might have been mitigated somewhat if laboring families had been able to continue to rely on cottage industries as a supplement to their earnings, but factory organization and production in the towns increasingly undercut these bye-employments.[83]

Changing terms of agrarian employment, especially in the southern counties, aggravated the effects of population growth. Before the latter part of the eighteenth century, it had been common for the larger farmers to provide room and board for some of their farm hands throughout the year. The "living-in" system, however, began to disappear as it lost its economic advantages for farmers. High wartime food prices after 1795, which increased the cost of board, and the advent of surplus labor, which made lodging unnecessary as a means of assuring an adequate labor supply, encouraged the conversion of farm servants into independent laborers working for wages.[84] The advent of surplus labor

---

[81] G.E. Mingay, Enclosure and the Small Farmer in the Age of the Industrial Revolution (London, 1968), p. 17.

[82] Jones, "The Agricultural Labour Market in England, 1793-1872," p. 325.

[83] W. Hasbach, A History of the English Agricultural Labourer (London, 1908), p. 137; A.W. Ashby, One Hundred Years of Poor Law Administration in a Warwickshire Village (Oxford, 1912), p. 34; Bovill, English Country Life, 1780-1830, p. 15. In some rural areas, certain domestic industries, such as straw-plaiting and glove- and lace-making, continued to hold important places in local economies.

[84] Minutes of the Select Committee of the House of Lords on the Poor Law, 1830-1, pp. 26-27; Inglis, Poverty and the Industrial Revolution, p. 47; Ernle,

spread its influence even further as the annual hiring of farm labor in general gave way to more casual hiring practices, the farmers often employing workers only on a daily basis as the need arose.[85] In short, traditional safeguards against deprivation were breaking down at the very moment the laborers were being caught in a wage-price squeeze.

Besides contributing to greater class differences in the countryside, this "proletarianization" of the agricultural laborers made larger numbers of the rural population more vulnerable to fluctuations in the agrarian economy. It is significant that the effects of these fluctuations were not general but were related to regional economic peculiarities. The arable-farming districts of the south and south-east posed the gravest problems. The relatively high labor requirements of arable farming and the large farms characteristic of this region encouraged an aggregation of agricultural workers.[86] The upshot was that there were generally more laborers per cultivated acre in the south and east than in other parts of England.[87]

English Farming Past and Present, p. 313; Hasbach, A History of the English Agricultural Labourer, pp. 176-77; Peacock, Bread or Blood, p. 24; Mingay, English Landed Society in the Eighteenth Century, pp. 240-41; Chambers and Mingay, The Agricultural Revolution, p. 112.

85 E.P. Thompson, The Making of the English Working Class (Harmondsworth, Middlesex, 1968), p. 235; Norman Gash, "Rural Unemployment, 1815-34," Economic History Review, VI (1935-6), p. 93; Chambers and Mingay, The Agricultural Revolution, p. 19; Hobsbawm and Rudé, Captain Swing, p. 44; Hampson, The Treatment of Poverty in Cambridgeshire, pp. 142-43; Clapham, An Economic History of Modern Britain: The Early Railway Age, pp. 121-22.

86 Hasbach, A History of the English Agricultural Labourer, p. 89; Chambers and Mingay, The Agricultural Revolution, p. 133.

87 See Tabular Statement Showing the Comparative Ability of the Several Counties in England to Support

However, because arable farming is by nature rhythmic in that its needs for labor vary at different times of the year, it was unable to offer stable employment outside planting and harvest time. Thus, the effects of the cyclical characteristics of arable farming and the concentrations of workers in those counties where it was practiced became critical when combined with the expansion of a casual, day-labor force: the result was seasonal unemployment and endemic underemployment at low wages.

In those areas where alternative employment opportunities existed, such as the manufacturing districts of the Midlands and the northern counties, the pressure on the poor was less acute, the urban centers drawing off some of the surplus labor.[88] It has been found that the effects of this process were regional rather than national, as the needs of industry were mostly met by short-distance migration.[89] In addition to encouraging the survival in northern agriculture of such institutions as "living-in" and payment in kind, the attraction of the towns helped to create an unmistakable disparity between farm wages in the north and south. In 1851, James Caird estimated that the weekly earnings of agricultural laborers in the manufacturing districts were about 37 percent higher than those of their counterparts in the more highly agricultural south.[90] In our period, a similar disparity prevailed, which was reflected in the distribution of pauperism in

---

Their Agricultural Population, P.P. (Lords), (58. of 1830-1), CCLXXXVII.

88 Arthur Redford, Labour Migration in England, 1800-50 (Manchester, 1926), p. 59.

89 Mark Blaug, "The Myth of the Old Poor Law and the Making of the New," Journal of Economic History, XXIII, 2 (1963), p. 169; Thompson, The Making of the English Working Class, p. 246; Redford, Labour Migration in England, p. 55; Chambers and Mingay, The Agricultural Revolution, p. 103.

90 Clapham, An Economic History of Modern Britain: The Early Railway Age, p. 466.

the country.[91] Appendix A, listing counties in order of poor relief expenditure per head of population for the year ending 25 March 1822 (picked at random), shows the extent to which pauperism was concentrated in the south and east.[92] If we differentiate counties on the basis of the famous Caird line running from the Severn to the Wash, which separated the northern high-wage counties from the low-wage counties of the south, the depressed condition of the southern laborers becomes even more apparent.[93] Leicestershire, the county with the highest per-capita relief expenditure of those north of the Caird line, does not appear on the list until 13th place, and even then the next most burdened county, Lincolnshire, occupies the 19th position. Indeed, only three of the fifteen counties and ridings north of the line appear in the first half of the list. It seems, then, that the greatest recourse to poor relief occurred in those areas where industrial development was too distant to exert an influence on a rural economy distinguished for surplus labor and substandard wages.[94]

Care must be taken in not overstating the speed and degree of change in rural life that led to social destabilization in the late-eighteenth and early-nineteenth centuries. The ratio of landless laboring families to families occupying land in Britain only rose from 2:1 in 1690 to 5:2 in 1831.[95] Even in Tudor

---

91 Blaug, "The Myth of the Old Poor Law and the Making of the New," p. 168.

92 Infra, p. 182. Notice also the low expenditure in the western pastoral counties.

93 A map indicating the location of the Caird line may be found in Blaug, "The Myth of the Old Poor Law and the Making of the New," p. 158.

94 Ibid., p. 170; D.C. Barnett, "Allotments and the Problem of Rural Poverty, 1780-1840," in Jones and Mingay, eds., Land, Labour and Population in the Industrial Revolution, p. 165.

95 J.H. Clapham, "The Growth of an Agrarian Proletariat, 1688-1832," Cambridge Historical Journal, I, 1 (1923), pp. 93-95.

times, large numbers of families, perhaps as many as two-thirds of England's households, received at least some part of their income from wages, and it had not been unusual for the husbandman's servant to become a day-laborer once he left his master's house to marry.[96] Rural society had also long been accustomed to "masterless" men outside the reach of paternalist control. Craftsmen of the manorial boroughs, isolated weavers and clothing workers, village artisans, colliers, bargees and carriers, millers, innkeepers, independent laborers, copyholders and squatters on the wastes, fishermen and smugglers on the coast, hunters in the forests, and denizens of the fenlands had been largely removed from the workings of genuine master-servant relationships. So too, chronic problems of underemployment were by no means new, property in the seventeenth century being hard put to find sufficient productive uses for an abundance of hands.[97] Still, the encroaching features of a free labor market became a serious social threat at that point when wages proved insufficient to support those who relied on them. The trend was clearly toward greater social instability as an enlarged work force became increasingly dependent on wages at a time when economic conditions were deteriorating for wage earners. In this regard, the rulers of rural society were faced with a series of crises that stretched over nearly half a century. The steep rise in food prices in the period from 1795 to 1813 was followed by falling wages after the Napoleonic Wars. This decline ended in 1824, after which real earnings of agricultural laborers remained somewhat steady until the 1840s when there was a slight reduction in some food prices. Over the country and the period as a whole, the effects of these price and wage movements remain a

---

[96] Laslett, The World We Have Lost, pp. 14-15, 17, 118.

[97] D.C. Coleman, "Labour in the English Economy of the 17th Century," Economic History Review, Second Series, VIII, 3 (1956), pp. 280-81, 289-90.

matter of interpretation, but the majority of laborers seem to have been better off in 1824 than they had been in 1790.[98] In the meantime, however, the gap between the high-wage counties of the north and the low-wage counties of the south had widened, and so in a number of southern areas it appears that the real income of the laborers actually declined in these years.[99]

The worsening situation in the south in the early-nineteenth century prompted the depressed agricultural laborers to protest on a scale that had been unknown in the eighteenth century.[100] In East Anglia, the reaction against local conditions was expressed for decades by almost continuous individual acts of violence in the form of incendiarism, cattle-maiming, fence-breaking, and so on.[101] These sporadic and localized protests were punctuated by upheavals of greater intensity and scope in 1800-01, 1816, 1830-31, and 1835-36. In particular, the Swing riots which swept southern and eastern England in 1830-31 stand out in vigor and latitude as a unique manifestation of despair.[102] It is also noteworthy that the altered circumstances of labor were reflected in the changing tactics of protest. Food rioting, which in the eighteenth century had expressed hostility toward middlemen and concern with grain prices, increasingly gave way to attacks on employers, participation in trade unions, and demands for higher wages and increased employment.[103]

---

98 Chambers and Mingay, The Agricultural Revolution, pp. 136-37.

99 Clapham, An Economic History of Modern Britain: The Early Railway Age, p. 129; Webb, English Poor Law History: The Last Hundred Years, Pt. II, Vol. I, p. 4.

100 Mingay, English Landed Society in the Eighteenth Century, p. 269; Dunbabin, Rural Discontent in Nineteenth-Century Britain, p. 18.

101 Peacock, "Village Radicalism in East Anglia, 1800-1850," pp. 27, 39.

102 Bovill, English Country Life, 1780-1830, p. 26.

103 Dunbabin, Rural Discontent in Nineteenth-Century Britain, p. 19; Hobsbawm and Rudé, Captain

Yet behind these upheavals was an attempt to restore a lost society which seemed to have more adequately safeguarded the subsistence of the laboring poor. The vestigial values of an older social order may be detected in the Swing rioters' demands for "fair wages" and "just prices" and their rejection of such innovations as wage-bargaining with employers.[104] Also revealing was their invocation of the authority of the magistrates, the monarch, or God for the actions they took.[105] In this way, riot was legitimized, the people assuming authority's proper role in order to enforce their customary rights to subsistence.[106] What is most salient here is popular insistence on the reciprocity of obligations inherent in the deference model. In one parish during the Swing disturbances, for example, the farmers agreed to an increase in wages if the laborers could persuade the parson to reduce his tithes. The laborers accordingly attended the tithe audit and were successful in forcing an abatement, following which a chronicler recorded that "we made our obedience to him [the parson] and he to us, and we gave him three cheers and went and set the Bells ringing and were all as pleased as could be at what we had done."[107] Once again we are sharply

---

Swing, p. 16; Rose, "Eighteenth Century Price Riots and Public Policy in England," p. 282; Thompson, "The Moral Economy of the English Crowd in the Eighteenth Century," p. 79.

104 G. Rudé, "English Rural and Urban Disturbances on the Eve of the First Reform Bill, 1830-1831," Past and Present, 37 (1967), p. 90.

105 Ibid., p. 90.

106 This had long been an aspect of "mob" action; in November 1693, large numbers of women seized grain from engrossers in several Oxfordshire towns, declaring that they were resolved "to put the law in execution since the magistrates neglected it." Quoted in Rose, "Eighteenth Century Price Riots and Public Policy in England," p. 280.

107 Quoted in Bovill, English Country Life, 1780-1830, p. 40. My emphasis.

reminded that obedience was not a ubiquitous or continuous feature of rural life. Because mutuality remained an essential part of community values, the readiness of subordinates to enforce popular expectations tempered a simple awe of authority. We see in these rural disturbances, in fact, the degree to which popular traditions could be a source of disruption when confronted with conditions that highlighted the derelictions of those who were held responsible for the protection of the humble.

This suggests that rural protest in this period was something more than a response to the material effects of population growth, changing terms of employment, and the decay of domestic industries. Also evident was the expression of a special sense of grievance because the norms of the community had not been matched by the behavior of those who had control over the necessities of life. This must call into question the usefulness of the deference model as a description of actual social relationships. As Eric Hobsbawm has recently reminded us, models derived from the history of culture become increasingly removed from realities during periods of swift, sustained, and fundamental change.[108] The prevalence of anonymous violence and major disturbances in the early-nineteenth century is itself indication enough of the failure of the rulers to provide the minimal requirements of the laborers. But more than this, an outright disregard for the welfare of the poor may be seen in such actions as the landowners' expropriation of commons and wastes and authority's attacks on the various use-rights of the people, which for centuries had provided some margin against want. Certainly the gentry's part in the brutal enforcement of the game laws, the destruction of housing for the creation of "close" parishes, and the economic rationalization of estate management should warn us against too readily ascribing to them a deep-seated sympathy for the poor.

---

108 Hobsbawm, "From Social History to the History of Society," p. 38.

It must be emphasized, nonetheless, that the ideal of an organic society continued to exert a hold on the minds of those who had the responsibility of governing rural England.[109] Among the foremost attractions of the order now rapidly passing were the possibilities it provided for the maintenance of social discipline.[110] The idea of the laborer as a tied-servant, an "unfree man," shielded against want and dependent upon his superiors for board and lodging, remained a compelling notion.[111] A select committee in 1828 urged the abolition of settlement by hiring and service, as it would be calculated "to revive that almost forgotten, but excellent practice, of domesticating the Agricultural Labourer in the establishment of his Employer, and thereby improve the moral feelings, industrious habits, and real comforts of the Poorer Classes."[112] This was an explicit appeal for the return to a vanished social and economic order, an order all the more alluring because it existed within the memory of many men.[113] Regardless of the part the landlords' own estate policies had played in the breakup of cherished institutions, they clung to an image of themselves as the protectors of the poor and charged their tenants with being insensitive to the plight of the laborers.[114] Even in those cases where such an image could only have been a delusion on the part of the landowners, at least the reassertion of appropriate role models continued to be seen as essential for the

---

109 J.D. Chambers, "The Making of the English Working Class," History, LI (1966), p. 183; Hobsbawm and Rudé, Captain Swing, pp. 61-62.

110 See, e.g., Peacock, Bread or Blood, p. 25.

111 Thompson, "Patrician Society, Plebian Culture," pp. 382-83.

112 Report [from the Select Committee] on the Law of Parochial Settlements, P.P., 1828, IV, p. 1.

113 Report on Labourers' Wages, 1824, p. 57.

114 Eric Richards, "'Captain Swing' in the West Midlands," International Review of Social History, XIX, 1 (1974), pp. 87-89.

justification of the social hierarchy. In other cases, the simple expression of proper values and modes of behavior went beyond a mere habit of social thinking and gave practical expression to paternal ideals. This was perhaps no more apparent than in the magistracy's administration of the poor laws.

III. Paternalism and the Old Poor Law

The very real need to alleviate widespread and prolonged distress among the laboring poor severely tested the effectiveness and depth of paternal benevolence in the late-eighteenth and early-nineteenth centuries. During the eighteenth century, it had often been impossible to detect in efforts to assist the poor where self-interested motives of social control left off and a genuine desire to improve their lot began, but by the turn of the century, the necessity of social conditioning was more generally appreciated.[1] From the 1790s, humanitarianism and evangelical piety, always strong elements in private philanthropy in the eighteenth century, were giving way to a more cynical and calculating approach to charity, animated by fear of the poor.[2] In view of the deteriorating conditions for significant segments of the rural population, it seemed more than ever essential to convince the laborers that they had an interest in the maintenance of the social order.[3] The subsistence crises of the 1790s were especially fruitful in producing schemes to ward off disaffection, such as the parochial subsidization of food prices, the establishment of public subscriptions, and stepped-up interference with the internal grain trade.[4] The poor laws, however, remained the most useful and pervasive instrument available to the

---

1 A.W. Coats, "Changing Attitudes to Labour in the Mid-Eighteenth Century," Economic History Review, Second Series, XI, 1 (1958), p. 36; idem, "Economic Thought and Poor Law Policy in the Eighteenth Century," pp. 42, 48-49.

2 David Owen, English Philanthropy, 1660-1960 (Cambridge, Mass., 1965), pp. 97-98.

3 Report on Labouring Poor (Allotments of Land), 1843, p. iv.

4 Thompson, "The Moral Economy of the English Crowd in the Eighteenth Century," p. 124; Chambers and Mingay, The Agricultural Revolution, p. 116.

provincial authorities in their efforts to encourage popular belief in the reality of paternal benevolence.[5] The importance of poor relief in the preservation of social equilibrium and discipline was so generally accepted that renewed outbreaks of incendiarism and disturbances in 1835 elicited local requests for assistance and advice from the newly-appointed poor law commissioners as well as the Home Office.[6]

Just how significant poor relief was in supporting the agricultural population is difficult to determine. A contemporary survey indicates that 9.7 percent of the country's population was in receipt of relief in 1831. A breakdown of percentages by counties reveals, as one would expect, an even greater reliance on the poor law system in the south, with Berkshire reporting 17 percent of its population on relief, Wiltshire 15 percent, Essex and Sussex 14 percent, Dorsetshire and Oxfordshire 13 percent, Buckinghamshire, Huntingdonshire, and Suffolk all over 12 percent, Cambridgeshire, Kent, Hertfordshire, Norfolk, and Northamptonshire 11 percent or more, and Herefordshire, Leicestershire, Bedfordshire, Shropshire, and Hampshire 10 percent or more.[7] In view of the primitive accounting techniques of the period and the propensity of overseers to count twice over those paupers who were relieved more than once, these figures must be treated with extreme care. Still, recent investigations have generally confirmed the existence of this level of aid dispensation.[8] One authority has even claimed that during the period between 1817 and 1821, perhaps more

---

[5] See, e.g., Thomas Mackay, A History of the English Poor Law (London, 1899), III, pp. 103-04.

[6] See First Annual Report [of the Poor Law Commissioners for England and Wales], P.P., 1835, XXXV, p. 9; Henry Pilkington/P[oor] L[aw] C[ommissioners], 10 July 1835, ibid., App. B, No. 9, p. 178.

[7] Tabular Statement Showing the Comparative Ability of the Several Counties in England to Support Their Agricultural Population, 1831.

[8] See Marshall, The Old Poor Law, 1795-1834, pp. 33, 36.

than 20 percent of the entire population received some relief.[9]

What this means in terms of able-bodied pauperism is less clear. We do know that 1795 -- a year of exceptionally severe and widespread food shortages and unemployment -- marked a permanent alteration in the pattern of poor relief.[10] Prior to this crisis, the parish pension lists were brief and made up chiefly of females, mostly widows, with a smattering of children, invalids, and old men. Then quite suddenly the lists lengthened, and the bulk of the new names were male, a situation that remained common right up to 1834. Arable farming's cyclical demand for labor proved to be a chronic problem for relief authorities. In the cereal-growing counties of the south and east, a select committee of 1828 found that from one-twelfth to one-fifth of the able-bodied laborers and their families were assisted from the rates "during several months of the year."[11] But averaging this dependence over entire counties does not convey a sense of the extent of able-bodied pauperism in some localities. There were many parishes, such as in the south of Wiltshire and parts of Sussex, Kent, Suffolk, and Cambridgeshire, where more than half the laboring families regularly received some poor relief during the year.[12] While it is true that at most periods the majority of laborers were not in receipt of aid, the instability in the labor market in many parts of the country always made the possibility

---

9 J.T. Krause, "Changes in English Fertility and Mortality, 1781-1850," Economic History Review, Second Series, XI, 1 (1958), p. 66.

10 G.W. Oxley, Poor Relief in England and Wales, 1601-1834 (Newton Abbot, Devon, 1974), pp. 112-13.

11 Report on the Employment or Relief of Able-Bodied Persons, 1828, p. 6.

12 Report [from the Select Committee] on Poor Rate Returns, P.P., 1825, IV, p. 22; Hobsbawm and Rudé, Captain Swing, pp. 73-74; Chambers and Mingay, The Agricultural Revolution, 1750-1880, p. 139; Gash, "Rural Unemployment, 1815-34," pp. 92-93.

of having to resort to the parish at some time very real for much of the agrarian population.[13]

During this period of increasing hardship for the poor, legislators in distant Westminster worked to amend the statute law pertaining to relief, giving the system a more humane and generous character.[14] Gilbert's Act of 1782 provided asylums for the impotent poor and encouraged the distribution of outdoor relief to the able-bodied; in the first years of the nineteenth century, acts were passed that withdrew power from local officials to badge paupers, to remove the sick, and to treat harshly mothers of illegitimate children, and statutes of 1796 and 1815 further extended outdoor relief; acts of 1814 and 1816 even rescinded the power of parochial authorities and workhouse masters to mete out punishment to paupers. As revealing as these acts are, they were only pale reflections of the changes then taking place in the actual administration of relief. A more significant indication of growing concerns for the state of the poor may be seen in the efforts of the bench to gain unrivalled control of the poor law system in the local communities. The advent of extensive magisterial intervention in parochial affairs is made all the more striking by the fact that for much of the eighteenth century the justices had tended to restrict their interference with local relief authorities in the exercise of their duties.[15]

Although the distribution of aid under the Old Poor Law was essentially a parochial responsibility, the system provided substantial opportunities for the magistrates to direct the administration of relief.

---

13 Marshall, The Old Poor Law, 1795-1834, p. 37. See C.R. Oldham, "Oxfordshire Poor Law Papers," Economic History Review, V, 1 (1934-35), p. 94.

14 Sidney and Beatrice Webb, English Poor Law History: The Old Poor Law (Hamden, Conn., 1963), Pt. I, pp. 422-23.

15 Thompson, "Patrician Society, Plebian Culture," p. 390; Ashby, One Hundred Years of Poor Law Administration in a Warwickshire Village, p. 40; Hampson, The Treatment of Poverty in Cambridgeshire, p. 225.

It is certainly not true that their intervention was restricted to the exercise of "only appellate jurisdiction."[16] By the end of the eighteenth century the quarter sessions, through means of committees of justices and a growing executive of salaried officials, had assumed important administrative, supervisory, and financial functions.[17] Since the sessions were not obliged to seek approval for their policies from the Home Secretary or any other higher authority, their discretion concerning affairs within their purview and jurisdictions was limited only by the personal views of the individual magistrates on the county bench.[18] It was in keeping with the local status of the magistracy that the collective decisions of the quarter sessions on relief matters were promulgated in the form of orders to the overseers of the poor.[19] At times of emergency the intervention of the county bench could be even more immediate and pervasive. In a procedure reminiscent of the 1630 Book of Orders, it was not unknown as late as the early-nineteenth century for quarter sessions to divide counties into districts under magisterial committees at whose weekly meetings relief was distributed to the poor.[20]

Corporate responsibility for directing relief administration was often rejected in favor of a more

personal control

---

[16] As is argued in Brundage, "The Landed Interest and the New Poor Law: A Reappraisal of the Revolution in Government," pp. 28, 34.

[17] Poynter, Society and Pauperism, p. 11.

[18] C.H.E. Zangerl, "The Social Composition of the County Magistracy in England and Wales, 1831-1887," Journal of British Studies, XI, 1 (1971), p. 114.

[19] M.D. Neuman, "A Suggestion Regarding the Origins of the Speenhamland Plan," English Historical Review, LXXXIV, 331 (1969), p. 321; Chambers, Nottinghamshire in the Eighteenth Century, pp. 73-74; Webb, English Poor Law History: The Old Poor Law, Pt. I, p. 181.

[20] Minutes of [Evidence Taken Before] the Lords Committee Appointed to Consider of the Poor Laws, P.P. (Lords), 1817, (43. of 1817), LXXIV, p. 91.

personal control of popular patronage. The primary concern of many magistrates in administering aid was not to maximize their power over wide areas, but to reaffirm their authority in the context of the local community.[21] This could result in the landlords assuming an even greater, more direct dominance over the relief machinery. Throughout the country, magisterial policy was enforced by means of a "rough and ready" organization of local petty sessions, consisting of two or three justices who met informally to supervise the parish officers.[22] The local sessions appointed, or at least approved, the overseers of the poor, who were then subject to the bench's direction even in the assessment of the rates.[23] In a manner similar to quarter sessional procedure, local gatherings of justices often prescribed by standing order the method of relief administration to be followed in the parishes under their jurisdiction.[24] The essence of such a system of administration was that the large proprietors, in the guise of magistrates, remained independent within their localities of larger jurisdictional entities, including the quarter sessions, whose decisions the individual justices did not always regard as binding.[25] There was, consequently, seldom any consistent or uniform

---

21 Infra, p. 65.

22 First Annual Report, 1835, pp. 4-5; G.E. Fussell, Village Life in the Eighteenth Century (Worcester, n.d.), pp. 24, 26; F.G. Emmison and I. Gray, County Records (London, 1967), p. 16; Tate, The Parish Chest, pp. 228-29; Hampson, The Treatment of Poverty in Cambridgeshire, pp. 228, 231; Poynter, Society and Pauperism, p. 11.

23 See Report on Poor Rate Returns, 1825, App. G, p. 22.

24 Report on Labourers' Wages, 1824, p. 23; Report [of the Poor Law Commissioners] on the Continuance of the Poor Law Commission, P.P., 1840, XVII, p. 12; Rose, The English Poor Law, 1780-1930, p. 57.

25 See, e.g., Report on the Poor Laws, 1817, pp. 90, 111.

relief policy enforced throughout any county for long.[26]

Because of this freedom from outside authority, the proprietors might dispense with even the pretense of legality in administering relief. The justices under the Old Poor Law repeatedly ignored statutes limiting the control of the bench to specific aspects of administration, and private meetings of local magistrates often proceeded without compunction to formulate extra-legal, and even illegal, policies pertaining to the amelioration of distress.[27] The formalities designed to ensure that the ratepayers' views and those of their officers were at least heard at the policy-making level were likewise sometimes not observed.[28] So complete was magisterial control in some districts that even when justices were aware that the enforcement of their policies went beyond their legal authority, they were not always deterred from insisting on the parish officers' compliance.[29]

Even where select vestries were established under the provisions of the Vestry Acts of 1818 and 1819, which were designed to induce economy in parish expenditure by restricting the intervention of the bench, the justices often remained unhampered in their activities. Although it required at least two magistrates to void a select vestry's decision, authority was given to one justice to order relief in cases of urgent need, the definition of which the magistrate himself determined.[30] The outright refusal of some magistrates to justify their orders for relief equally rendered

---

26 Webb, English Poor Law History: The Old Poor Law, Pt. I, p. 426.

27 First Annual Report, 1835, pp. 4-5; Hampson, The Treatment of Poverty in Cambridgeshire, p. 228.

28 Minutes of the Lords Committee Appointed to Consider of the Poor Laws, 1817, p. 65; Webb, English Poor Law History: The Old Poor Law, Pt. I, pp. 168-69.

29 Report on Labourers' Wages, 1824, p. 35.

30 Report on the Employment or Relief of Able-Bodied Persons, 1828, p. 5. Since the justices acted most often in petty sessions, such limitations were not usually relevant in any event.

these measures ineffective.[31] Complaints received by the House of Commons in the 1820s from parishes in Lincolnshire, Oxfordshire, Shropshire, Somersetshire, Durham, Cornwall, and the North Riding attest to the ability and inclination of justices to dictate the relief policy of many select vestries.[32] The magistrates' successful opposition in the same period to even the establishment of such bodies in Northamptonshire, Nottinghamshire, Somersetshire, and Cambridgeshire reveals even more dramatically the power of the justices to counter parochial attempts to control relief policy through the administration of ratepayers in select vestries.[33]

These scattered examples in the Parliamentary Papers suggest that we would be likely to find fewer select vestries in the distressed districts, where the magistrates were most intent on retaining their grasp on relief administration. The distribution figures for the entire country appear to confirm this expectation. As of 25 March 1823 there were 2,452 select vestries in the 41 counties and ridings of England. Nearly one-half of these bodies (1,220) were located in the 15 counties and ridings north of the Caird high-wage line; Cheshire, Lancashire, and Yorkshire alone accounted for 611 select vestries, or about 25 percent

---

31 [Report from His Majesty's Commissioners for Inquiring into the Administration and Practical Operation of the Poor Laws, App. B.1], Answers to Rural Queries, P.P., 1834, XXXIII, p. 73d; Report [from the Select Committee] on Poor Rate Returns, P.P., 1822, V, p. 8; Report [from the Select Committee] on Poor Rate Returns, P.P., 1824, VI, App. F.1, p. 19.

32 Report [from the Select Committee] on Poor Rate Returns, P.P., 1823, V, App. E, pp. 16, 17; Reports on Poor Rate Returns, 1822, App. E, p. 29; 1824, App. F.1, p. 19; 1825, App. G, pp. 17, 21.

33 Reports on Poor Rate Returns, 1823, App. E, pp. 17-18; 1825, App. G, p. 21; Hampson, The Treatment of Poverty in Cambridgeshire, p. 246.

of the total for all of England.[34] This means that 1,232 select vestries were shared among the more numerous counties south of the Caird line, which resulted in lower concentrations of select vestries in this region, Bedfordshire, for example, having only 12, Berkshire 25, Cambridgeshire 17, Hertfordshire 18, Huntingdonshire 11, Middlesex 15, Surrey 21, and Wiltshire 29. It may not be claimed without more complete evidence that this relative paucity of select vestries in the southern counties was entirely owing to magisterial opposition to their formation. Nevertheless, it is fair to say that in those districts where the justices were most concerned with relief administration, the ratepayers were least able to combat magisterial interference through the use of statutory authorities that envisaged tighter ratepayer control of aid dispensation. The ineffectiveness of the vestry system as a real challenge to the accustomed influence of the landowners is especially evident in view of the fact that the greater proportion of the parishes that adopted select-vestry administration were those with large populations, those which regardless of organizational forms had often managed in any event to maintain a semblance of independence.[35]

The appellate jurisdiction of the magistrates -- what an 1828 select committee called "an indirect but effectual power"[36] -- also provided the bench with a considerable and far-ranging means of directing parochial administration. Under the Old Poor Law, the responsibility of the landowners to ensure the laborers' subsistence was recognized in the right of the poor to

---

[34] Report on Poor Rate Returns, 1824, App. B, p. 8. The county in this group with the lowest number of select vestries, Nottinghamshire, had 31.

[35] Report on Poor Rate Returns, 1823, p. 5; Third Annual Report [of the Poor Law Commissioners for England and Wales], P.P., 1837, XXXI, p. 13; Ashby, One Hundred Years of Poor Law Administration in a Warwickshire Village, p. 44.

[36] Report on the Employment or Relief of Able-Bodied Persons, 1828, p. 4.

appeal to the bench against the relief decisions of the overseers and the ratepayers in vestries.[37] Since the appellate procedure could involve onerous duties for the overseers, such as the need to travel many miles to the nearest magistrates to justify their actions, the appeals of the paupers were many times conceded by default.[38] In other cases, the poor were able to extract more generous relief from the overseers by merely threatening to take them before the bench, because of either the habitual reluctance of the overseers to confront the justices or the propensity of the magistrates to override the parish officers.[39] The result was that overseers tended to anticipate probable orders from the local justices without the bench having to intervene formally.[40]

The justices' appellate jurisdiction was such a highly potent means of intervention because its utilization extended beyond parish boundaries and was not confined to the range of the magistrates' immediate personal influence.[41] A survey made by the Royal Commission of Inquiry in 1832 shows that even populous rural centers lacking a major landowner, the so-called open parishes, were not outside the reach or concern of

---

37 Ibid., p. 5.

38 Report on the Poor Laws, 1817, p. 23; Webb, English Poor Law History: The Old Poor Law, Pt. I, p. 162.

39 Minutes of the Lords Committee Appointed to Consider of the Poor Laws, 1817, p. 88; Report on Poor Rate Returns, 1823, App. E, p. 18; S.G. and E.O.A. Checkland, Introduction, P.L.C. Report of 1834, Pelican edn., p. 37.

40 Ibid., p. 37; Report on the Employment or Relief of Able-Bodied Persons, 1828, p. 22.

41 Richard Earle/P.L.C., 25 June 1836, Second Annual Report [of the Poor Law Commissioners for England and Wales], P.P., 1836, XXIX, App. B, No. 15, p. 387; Minutes of Evidence of the Select Committee of the House of Lords Appointed to Consider of the Poor Laws, 1830-31, pp. 3, 58-59; Report on the Employment or Relief of Able-Bodied Persons, 1828, p. 55.

the bench.[42] One of the chief complaints voiced in the replies to the survey was that magistrates residing at a distance controlled parochial administration through the issuance of orders on appeal or the threat of calling the overseers before them. It only required a readiness among the poor of the "open" parishes to resort to the neighboring justices in order to bring the parochial authorities into line with the surrounding proprietors' views on relief administration. In some instances, an actual appeal did not even have to be granted, the overseers conforming to what was taken to be magisterial policy on the basis of other parishes' experience with justices in the district.[43]

There is a need here, of course, to determine as nearly as possible the extent of magisterial meddling in the early-nineteenth century. Thanks to the Royal Commission of Inquiry such a task is not entirely unrealistic, for this body collected some rather extensive evidence of magisterial activities. In 1832, the commissioners drew up a set of queries which was distributed to selected rural relief officials. Replies were received from more than 10 percent of the 15,000 parishes in England and Wales, representing approximately 20 percent of the entire population. Fortunately, question 43 of that circular was directed to the issue that concerns us here. Local authorities were asked: "Is Relief or Allowance generally given in consequence of the advice or order of the Magistrates, or under the opinion that the Magistrates would make an Order for it if application were made to them?" A compilation of the answers the commission received is found in Appendix B.[44]

Before evaluating this tabulation certain points should be clarified. Because the respondents were free

---

[42] See Answers to Rural Queries, 1834, qq. 43 and 44, _passim_.

[43] _Report on the Employment or Relief of Able-Bodied Persons_, 1828, p. 28; _First Annual Report_, 1835, p. 12.

[44] _Infra_, pp. 183-84.

to answer as they pleased, the replies were often ambiguous or irrelevant, and it was not unusual for the question to go unanswered altogether. Of the 1,170 English parishes responding to the survey, 386 did not answer the question or made an irrelevant reply; these responses have not been taken into consideration in computing the percentages in columns 6, 7, and 8 of the tabulation. Also, it is not clear on what basis the reporting parishes were selected, so it must not be assumed that they represent a random sample of all rural parishes. On the other hand, there is no suggestion that the reporting parishes were chosen with any special criteria in mind, and despite the shortcomings of the survey, it does provide a valuable glimpse into relief administration in a large number of parishes.[45] This may be seen from a breakdown of the replies to question 43 for the whole of England: 488 parishes reported that relief was distributed according to the directions of the justices, 235 that it was not, and 61 that the bench sometimes interfered.

Even if these results only just approximate reality, they are a significant indication that by 1832 the English justice of the peace was no stranger to the operation of the poor laws. In 66 percent (27) of the 41 counties and ridings the bench directly controlled relief policy in half or more of the reporting parishes. In 34 percent (14) of the counties and ridings the magistrates dictated policy in two-thirds or more of the parishes making returns. Only in 29 percent (12) of the counties and ridings were half or more of the reporting parishes entirely free from such interference. It should be noted that these figures include counties in the west Midlands and the north where there was a particularly low level of intervention, the West Riding being an interesting exception. If atten-

---

[45] Mark Blaug has used this same survey as the basis for some significant conclusions regarding relief practices prior to 1834. See "The Poor Law Report Reexamined," Journal of Economic History, XXIV (1964), pp. 229-45.

tion is confined to the southern and eastern districts, the area of the country suffering from the most acute agrarian distress, a much more impressive indication of magisterial activity is found. In some counties, such as Sussex, Buckinghamshire, Essex, Oxfordshire, Northamptonshire, Wiltshire, Berkshire, Huntingdonshire, Hampshire, Dorsetshire, Surrey, and Somersetshire, all recording "yes" replies of over 70 percent, the bench seems to have been particularly active. Clearly a pattern of intervention based on the degree of rural distress emerges from the tabulation. It should be noticed that the counties listed in the appendix are ranked according to poor relief expenditure for 1831, with the most burdened county, Sussex, appearing at the head of the chart (see column 5). In the first 21 counties listed, 18 record unequivocal magisterial interference in half or more of their reporting parishes, while in the next 20 counties listed, only 9 record a similar level of magisterial activity (see column 6). This suggests that the justices were most heavily involved in the administration of relief in those districts where the pressure of poverty and the burden on the rates were greatest, deteriorating conditions for the poor most often prompting magisterial action.

It may be that the Swing riots of 1830 in southern and southeastern England had led to an increased need to show interest in the welfare of the laborers in those areas. But it would be a mistake to view these disturbances as an isolated event, producing a unique flurry of concern among the gentry. The general tumults of 1795 and 1800-01, the East Anglian risings of 1816 and 1822, and the increase in rural crime and sporadic violence after 1815 showed clearly enough over a long period of time the depth of the crisis of poverty and the need for the authorities to act.[46] The rash of parliamentary investigations of the poor laws that followed the Napoleonic Wars reveals an unmistakable determination among the justices to secure

---

[46] Hobsbawm and Rudé, Captain Swing, pp. 77-80.

control of the increasingly important administration of the poor laws. A select committee in 1828 noted that "in many counties, . . . especially throughout the South of England," the justices had assumed the responsibility of directing relief administration, particularly as it affected the able-bodied poor and their families.[47] The reports of other bodies in the years leading up to 1828 give substantial support for such a claim, select committees in 1822, 1823, 1824, 1825, and 1826 finding that the bench was active in intruding into parochial affairs.[48]

The rapid spread after 1795 of the allowance system, a method of wage subsidization from the poor rates commonly known as the Speenhamland plan, also indicates the degree to which the bench had become involved in relief administration, for this technique of aid dispensation was nearly always associated with sessional decisions. Allowances in aid of wages appear to have had their greatest vogue during the Napoleonic Wars, with a decline in their use setting in after high wartime grain prices had collapsed.[49] Notwithstanding this, select committees found evidence of the continued use of the allowance system in parts of Suffolk, Sussex, Bedfordshire, Buckinghamshire, Dorsetshire, Wiltshire, Norfolk, Huntingdonshire, Devonshire, Kent, Hertford-

---

47 Report on the Employment or Relief of Able-Bodied Persons, 1828, p. 4.

48 Reports on Poor Rate Returns, 1822, App. E, pp. 28, 38; 1823, App. E, pp. 27-29; 1825, App. G, p. 20; Report on Labourers' Wages, 1824, p. 6; Report [from the Select Committee] on Poor Rate Returns, P.P., 1826, III, App. F, pp. 17-18.

49 Blaug, "The Poor Law Report Reexamined," p. 231; idem, "The Myth of the Old Poor Law and the Making of the New," pp. 159, 166. On the other hand, a recent study by D.A. Baugh suggests that the bench may well have been engaged in extending, rather than abandoning, the use of allowance scales in the years after the war. "The Cost of Poor Relief in South-East England, 1790-1834," Economic History Review, Second Series, XXVIII (1975), p. 64.

shire, Hampshire, Surrey, Essex, Cambridgeshire, Middlesex, Berkshire, and Oxfordshire as late as 1828.[50] It should be stressed, however, that the intervention of the magistrates in these years was not confined to the mere adoption of allowance scales in sessional meetings. A significant point of the 1832 survey is that even at the time the allowance system is believed to have "generally disappeared,"[51] the justices remained an essential, if not the pivotal, part of the poor relief system in southern England.

The findings of a host of select committees, then, serve to support and confirm the more detailed view of local administration provided by the answers to the royal commission's rural queries. While this material precludes the precision in interpretation that can often be achieved through grass-roots research on original parish documents, these contemporary investigations probably represent the most decisive evidence available in connection with the role and influence of the large landowners in the pre-reform relief system. Any effort simply to correlate formal sessional decisions, especially those made at the county level, with actual administration in the parishes will fail to account for the highly personal and diversified nature of magisterial policy-making under the Old Poor Law.[52] The individual magnates holding sway in their own parishes without reference to any outside authority, the readiness of the laborers to resort to appeals to the local bench, and the overseers' tendency to anticipate magisterial judgements, particularly if threatened with an appearance before the justices, all constituted

---

[50] Report on Labourers' Wages, 1824, p. 5; Abstract of Returns Made to the Committee in 1824 Relative to Labourers' Wages, P.P., 1825, XIX, passim; Report on the Employment or Relief of Able-Bodied Persons, 1828, p. 5.

[51] Blaug, "The Poor Law Report Reexamined," p. 231.

[52] For such an attempt, see M.D. Neuman, "Speenhamland in Berkshire," in E.W. Martin, ed., Comparative Development in Social Welfare (London, 1972), pp. 107-10.

what may be termed the "invisible influence" of the magistrates in poor relief affairs. Consequently, their authority in relief administration may not always be assessed in terms of the volume and scope of their formal decisions in sessions; indeed, the situation might arise where magisterial influence may actually appear to have been diminishing at the very time it was, in fact, increasing.

This does not mean that the magistrates were entirely free to conduct the relief system according to their perceptions of the needs of local administration. The distribution of the poor rates signified far more than the machinations of government, whether national or local, and, of course, embodied more than the sum of the myriad of statutes and court decisions that constituted the legal and official framework of the poor laws. Customary usages pertaining to relief often conditioned administration, especially as the laboring poor came to adopt them as part of their rights and heritage. The distribution of public funds was popularly conceived to be the means by which, in the last extremity, the local society discharged its obligation to support all of its members.[53] Parochial authorities reported that the laborers regarded relief as their fair share of the social dividend, a select committee in 1824 noting that on the justices' allowance "the labourer relies as a right; and when he receives less, he makes an angry appeal to a Magistrate, not as a petitioner for charity, but as a claimant for justice. . . ."[54] Within this milieu, the authorities often had little choice but to conform to the roles expected of them as community leaders. County magistrates told two select committees in 1817 and one in 1824 that the granting of aid on appeal was commonly considered to be "imperative upon

---

[53] Webb, English Poor Law History: The Old Poor Law, Pt. I, pp. 181-82.

[54] Report on Labourers' Wages, 1824, p. 7. See also Report on the Employment or Relief of Able-Bodied Persons, 1828, p. 27.

the Magistrate. . . ."[55] Practical weight was added to these expectations by the laborers' readiness to resort to violence in order to obtain their rights in the poor's rate, as was repeatedly the case in East Anglia throughout the pre-reform period.[56] There was, to be sure, the safety valve of the laborers' prerogative to appeal to the community's leaders for a redress of grievances, but even this procedure could at times assume a sufficiently menacing aspect.[57] The report of a Bedfordshire magistrate to the poor law commissioners provides an example of how the appellate procedure could result in the virtual coercion of the authorities if those seeking to economize at the poor's expense tampered with relief on any significant scale: "In one Parish in the County, the Overseers having decided that the able-bodied . . . should not be paid more than 1/4 in Money, & the rest in Provisions, the Applicants refused these terms, and immediately went in considerable numbers (above 200) to an adjoining Magistrate . . . In consequence of this a Meeting of the Magistrates in the district was immediately convened and the Overseers were required not to act upon the System."[58] Even those justices who preferred to leave relief matters to their subordinates often found that they could not disengage themselves from parish affairs, as the bench quite obviously had to deal in some way with all complainant initiatives. In this way, economic pressures on the laborers helped to transform the magistrates' administration of the poor laws. Once a

---

[55] Minutes of the Lords Committee Appointed to Consider of the Poor Laws, 1817, p. 19; Report on the Poor Laws, 1817, p. 90; Report on Labourers' Wages, 1824, p. 34.

[56] Peacock, "Village Radicalism in East Anglia, 1800-50," p. 36.

[57] See, e.g., Minutes of Evidence of the Select Committee of the House of Lords Appointed to Consider of the Poor Laws, 1830-31, p. 8.

[58] Bedford Union: George P. Livens/P.L.C., 24 October 1834, M.H. 12/21.

part of the body of communal rituals primarily designed to highlight the power and authority of rulers -- what Edward Thompson calls "the theater of the great"[59] -- the magistrates' role in administration now required close attention to the day-to-day operation of a social institution of increased scope and significance in the community.

Admittedly, demonstrating the interference of the bench in poor law administration does not necessarily show that that interference was consistently exercised on behalf of the poor. This becomes especially clear in light of recent arguments that the bulk of the justices came to adopt an unsympathetic posture in regard to the distribution of relief during the last decades of the Old Poor Law, the magisterial opponent of parochial attempts to reduce the rates being a "black sheep," defying "the consensus of the local landed magnates."[60] It may, in fact, be stated with some confidence that from about 1795 onwards, the intervention of the magistracy was often systematically directed toward undermining parish economy measures, most notably in the rural parishes of southern England.[61] Throughout the period before the reform of the poor laws in 1834, there was a general belief that only a parish free from the influence of the bench was able to reduce its rates to the level desired by most parishioners.[62] Even when faced with declining rents in the years after Waterloo,

---

[59] See Thompson, "Patrician Society, Plebian Culture," pp. 390, 397.

[60] A. Brundage, "The English Poor Law of 1834 and the Cohesion of Agricultural Society," Agricultural History, XLVIII, 3 (1974), pp. 407-08; idem, "The Landed Interest and the New Poor Law: A Reply," pp. 347-48.

[61] Report on Labourers' Wages, 1824, p. 6. See Rose, The English Poor Law, 1834-1930, p. 38; Webb, English Poor Law History: The Old Poor Law, Pt. I, p. 166.

[62] See, e.g., Report on the Poor Laws, 1817, p. 76; Report on Poor Rate Returns, 1823, p. 16.

the magistrates widely refrained from using their statutory power (under 50 Geo. III, c. 49) to reduce overseers' accounts.[63] In later years the justices continued to be regarded as the main obstacle to efforts to economize; Nassau Senior informed Lord Brougham in 1832 that the magistrates as a group opposed all measures that would too severely constrict aid distribution:

> . . . the resident landlords are generally either farmers or magistrates; and the means of obtaining popularity and exerting influence which the present system gives to the magistrates seem to be, with most of them, superior to every other consideration. They appear also . . . to be actuated by an <u>esprit de corps</u> more intense than that of any other class of functionaries . . . I have no hope of real improvement [i.e., a reduction in rates] while their power of interference remains undiminished. . . .[64]

The royal commission's 1832 survey also shows unequivocal magisterial support for more generous relief on the eve of reform. The survey leaves the distinct sense that the justices almost invariably provided the barrier between the poor and the ratepayers in vestries who wished to scale down the rates. A simple quantification of the answers to question 44 of the rural queries confirms this impression. Question 44 asked: "What do you think would be the effect, immediate and ultimate, of making the decision of the Vestry or Select

---

63 <u>Report on Poor Rate Returns</u>, 1822, p. 7. See Tate, <u>The Parish Chest</u>, p. 17.

64 N.W. Senior/Lord Brougham, 14 September 1832, in S. Leon Levy, <u>Nassau W. Senior, 1790-1864</u> (Newton Abbot, Devon, 1970), App. X, p. 249. See also Richard Earle/P.L.C., 25 June 1836, <u>Second Annual Report</u>, 1836, App. B, No. 15, p. 386.

Vestry in matters of Relief final?" Of the 291 respondents who specifically addressed themselves to the issue of the probable level of relief expenditure under unrestricted vestry control, 272 believed that circumventing magisterial influence would mean a more stringent and economical distribution of aid, while only 10 maintained that relief would be dispensed more lavishly.[65]

There is the possibility that efforts to counter parish economy measures were the work of scattered "maverick J.P.s" rather than large segments of the magistracy.[66] The chance of individual, lone "poor men's justices" disregarding the views of their colleagues while directing relief administration over wide areas must be taken seriously, if only because one of the assistants to the royal commission claimed this to be the case.[67] The replies to the commission's own survey, however, do not bear out this view. Of the 488 parishes reporting that the bench controlled relief administration, 328 gave some indication of whether the magistrates intervened singly or in groups. Of these, 302 reported interference by two or more justices, while only 26 noted a solitary justice intruding into relief affairs. Moreover, this latter group of magistrates appears to have intervened singly only in those areas under their direct social and economic influence, for in only two cases is there a clear example of a lone justice meddling in a parish outside his personal control. Consequently, it seems that when parochial authorities were interfered with, it was almost always the work of two or more magistrates sit-

---

[65] Nine asserted that there would be no change. Many more parishes than this actually answered the question, but their comments are irrelevant to the matter under consideration here.

[66] Brundage, "The English Poor Law of 1834 and the Cohesion of Agricultural Society," p. 407; idem, "The Landed Interest and the New Poor Law: A Reply," p. 348.

[67] P.L.C. Report of 1834, Pelican edn., pp. 229-30. Also quoted in Brundage, "The Landed Interest and the New Poor Law: A Reply," p. 348.

ting in petty sessions. There is, in any event, no evidence here of a handful of actively compassionate or fearful justices frustrating large numbers of non-interventionist magistrates, who wished to support economy measures. The interference of the bench was simply too common a feature of parochial administration, too widespread, and its tendency too unmistakable to accept the validity of such a notion.

One factor that may lead to a supposition of magisterial support for a more stringent distribution of aid was the reduction in minimum bread rations established by quarter sessions in the years after the Napoleonic Wars.[68] Many of the sessional relief scales from this period were less generous than those which had been in general use in the south some twenty years earlier; this was true of the Northamptonshire scale of 1816, the Cambridgeshire and Essex scales of 1821, a Wiltshire scale of 1817, a Hampshire scale of 1822, and the Dorsetshire scale of 1826.[69] In evaluating the significance of this decline it must be stressed once again that formal bread scales do not adequately reflect the ad hoc, local nature of poor law administration in the period before 1834. Many justices considered the quarter sessions to be an inappropriate body for the formulation of poor law policy because of the special concerns of the landlords in each of the parishes under their local jurisdiction.[70] In a relief system notorious for its heterogeneity, it is not surprising that the qualities of precision, permanence, and uniformity associated with the word Speenhamland were rarely found. The point is that bread scales do not always provide an accurate view of practice at local, parish level.[71] In addition, the

---

[68] Michael Brock, The Great Reform Act (London, 1973), p. 124; Blaug, "The Myth of the Old Poor Law and the Making of the New," pp. 161-62; Brundage, "The Landed Interest and the New Poor Law: A Reply," p. 347.

[69] Hammond, The Village Labourer, pp. 184-85.

[70] Answers to Rural Queries, 1834, XXXIII, q. 44, passim.

[71] See Neuman, "Speenhamland in Berkshire,"

bread scales were becoming less important for the support of the poor just at the time scales were declining in generosity. High bread prices, the chief concern of relief authorities in the first two decades of the nineteenth century, forced attention on the need to ensure an adequate wage for subsistence. By the 1820s, however, prices were lower, which rendered the scale allowance less critical (except for laborers with large families), while the problems of structural and seasonal unemployment were more strongly felt, requiring more direct means of magisterial intervention than the setting of bread scales.[72]

Still, there is no doubt that official relief scales published after 1815 were not as generous as the original Speenhamland model. It would be foolhardy, nonetheless, to attribute this fact simply to a consensus among the magistrates that economy should be pursued at the poor's expense. It is true that many of those in authority had come to question the social value of distributing public aid, and criticism of the relief system certainly increased in this period. At a time of falling profits for agriculture as a result of a steep decline in grain prices after 1813, it is also true that landowners had become concerned about the effect of the rate burden on the ability of their tenants to pay rents. On the other hand, there is an abundance of evidence that it was growing dissatisfaction among the ratepayers that forced the justices into a more careful distribution of aid. If nothing else, the responses to question 44 of the rural queries reveal the strength of pressures to economize that the bench faced (and resisted) in this period. In attempting to control the mechanisms of relief dispensation, the southern magistrates often encountered sullen opposition from the smaller tenant and freehold

---

pp. 107-08.

[72] Oxley, Poor Relief in England and Wales, 1601-1834, pp. 116-17; Baugh, "The Cost of Poor Relief in South-East England, 1790-1834," pp. 59-64.

farmers, who bore the brunt of declining prices and rising rates. This could not help but influence magisterial actions, as the Rev. Philip Hunt, a Bedfordshire magistrate, made clear in his testimony before a select committee in 1824: "The pressure of the times has been such, and in some parishes the poor rates were levied with so much difficulty, that magistrates have restricted their relief to what was absolutely required for the support of the family. . . ."[73]

After 1815 it became well-nigh official policy to discriminate between the "deserving" and "undeserving" poor when distributing the rates, select committees of the House of Commons in 1817, 1819, and 1824 urging local authorities to consider the character of the applicant before granting an appeal.[74] But when laborers in many parts of the country were pressed so closely to utter destitution, when any disruption in relief promised to drive the poor below the margin of subsistence, such exhortations were largely unrealistic. "I have found on many Occasions," William Wilshere, magistrate of Hertfordshire and Bedfordshire, told an 1817 committee, "that I have been compelled to order Relief for those whose Distress has arisen from their own gross Improvidence; but I nevertheless felt that I was bound to order it; that they could not perish."[75] Wilshere's testimony was supported by that of William Sherbrooke, a Nottinghamshire J.P., who reported that the magistrate was "obliged" to order relief "unless he will see that Family starve. . . ."[76] When questioned before the 1824 committee on laborers' wages,

---

[73] _Report on Labourers' Wages_, 1824, p. 40.

[74] _Report on the Poor Laws_, 1817, pp. 22-23; _Report [from the Select Committee] on the Poor Laws_, P.P., 1819, II, pp. 3-4; _Report on Labourers' Wages_, 1824, p. 8. See also Poynter, _Society and Pauperism_, p. 43.

[75] _Minutes of the Lords Committee Appointed to Consider of the Poor Laws_, 1817, p. 25.

[76] _Ibid._, p. 97.

the Rev. Philip Hunt indicated a similar lack of alternatives available to the magistrates when confronted with those suffering from dire poverty:

> Is the character of the labourer taken into consideration when . . . relief is ordered? -- No; for the scale is calculated merely as to what is absolutely necessary for support or maintenance.
>
> It is entirely intended then for the mere subsistence of the labourer and his family? -- For the mere subsistence of the labourer and his family, without any reference to the moral character of the individuals that compose that family.[77]

Even the Suffolk justices, who fully sympathized with the plight of the small ratepayers, felt the bench was powerless to reject appeals of the poor for aid. In a memorial sent to the 1817 select committee on the poor laws, the Suffolk Quarter Sessions declared that "if the labourer, whose earnings are insufficient for his support, applies to a magistrate, the magistrate, having no power to fix the rate of wages, MUST, however reluctantly, ORDER relief from the Poor Rate; and, as this order is final and conclusive, the several classes . . . aggrieved by this unequal assessment [the small ratepayers], are precluded from the benefit of appeal against the overseers account, and left without remedy. . . ."[78]

The point to bear in mind from all of this is

---

77 Report on Labourers' Wages, 1824, p. 35. My emphasis.

78 Memorial of the Magistrates of the County of Suffolk, respecting Poor Rates, n.d., in Report on the Poor Laws, 1817, App. H., p. 167. Original emphasis. The petition was signed by Lord Rous and fourteen other justices.

that even those justices who wished to respond to the demands of the ratepayers could only go so far in reducing relief, for the bench was hemmed in by the desperation of the poor and the needs of social discipline. The result was that the magistrates might have been willing to sanction reductions in aid to the point where it provided only what was absolutely required for subsistence. But when the laborers were threatened with extreme want, the justices very often showed themselves resolved to thwart parochial efforts to drive down relief even further. The diminution of relief in the post-war period thus represented what was seen as a necessary adjustment in magisterial policy rather than a move to lend full support to the economy measures of hard-pressed ratepayers. This explains the apparent contradiction between declining relief scales after 1815 and the evidence of parliamentary investigations and official surveys that the local justices nearly always intervened in favor of the poor, and did so in strength at times of deteriorating conditions for the laborers. Relief allotments, in short, could reach the level where the community leaders felt bound to oppose the economic interests of their rate-paying constituents.

What the ratepayers failed or refused to appreciate was that the magistrates had so few options in ordering relief once quarter sessions or the parochial authorities had reduced relief to the subsistence level. The almost invariable ratepayer predilection, at least as it is expressed in the Parliamentary Papers, was to differentiate between the "deserving" and "undeserving" poor when distributing the rates.[79]

---

[79] See Minutes of the Lords Committee Appointed to Consider of the Poor Laws, 1817, pp. 35-36; Report on the Poor Laws, 1817, p. 109; Report on Poor Rate Returns, 1824, App. F.1, p. 17; Report on Poor Rate Returns, 1825, App. G, p. 18; James P. Huzel, "Malthus, the Poor Law, and Population in Early-Nineteenth-Century England," Economic History Review, Second Series, XXII, 3 (1969), p. 446.

Any overt deviation from such a principle was almost certain to elicit a stream of protests from ratepayers that the appeal procedure operated as "a premium for profligacy" and resulted in the moral degeneration of the laborers.[80] This may be seen in the widespread dissatisfaction of ratepayers with magisterial administration which select committees first uncovered in the 1820s, and which was more systematically confirmed by the 1832 rural queries, the royal commission receiving, according to Nassau Senior, "many complaints of the conduct of magistrates."[81] The remarks of the Rev. Joseph Bosworth, vicar of Little Horwood, Buckinghamshire, may serve to sum up the resulting dilemma that confronted the bench in its administration of relief: "The minimum [allowance] of the magistrates is the maximum of the farmers."[82] Within this broad context of differing opinions, the sources of local conflict and animosities were multitudinous.

This meant that magisterial control of the relief system was made all the more difficult if ratepayers should ever be in a position to make their influence felt.[83] The dramatic change in relief prac-

---

80 See Board of Agriculture, The Agricultural State of the Kingdom (New York, 1970. Original edn., 1816), p. 25; Reports on Poor Rate Returns, 1822, App. E, pp. 28-30; 1824, App. F.2, p. 25; 1825, App. G, p. 19; 1826, App. F, pp. 17-18.

81 N. Senior/Lord Brougham, 14 September 1832, in Levy, Nassau W. Senior, 1790-1864, App. X, p. 247; Richard Hall/P.L.C., 10 July 1835, First Annual Report, App. B, No. 4, p. 129; P.L.C. Report of 1834, Pelican edn., p. 240. See Reports on Poor Rate Returns, 1822, App. E, pp. 28-30; 1824, App. F.2, p. 25; 1825, App. G, p. 19; 1826, App. F, pp. 17-18; Minutes of the Lords Committee Appointed to Consider of the Poor Laws, 1817, p. 74.

82 Report on the Employment or Relief of Able-Bodied Persons, 1828, p. 38.

83 See Report on Poor Rate Returns, 1823, App. E, p. 18; Report on the Poor Laws, 1817, p. 82; Hampson, The Treatment of Poverty in Cambridgeshire, p. 246.

tices in many parishes following the reform of the poor laws in 1834 attests to the distinct and prevalent desire of most ratepayers to run their affairs according to what they conceived to be their own best interests. Although themselves prominent advocates of a more stringent administration of relief, the poor law commissioners appointed under the amending act were horrified to find occurrences of a "precipitate and violent change [in aid dispensation] made by some of the overseers on their own responsibility" during the transition in modes of relief administration. "[We] found," the commissioners stated in their first annual report, "that a conception had been extensively propagated amongst the overseers in the rural parishes . . . that by the operation of the Poor Law Amendment Act they were entirely released from the control of the magistrates. The consequences . . . were represented to be, that those dependent on parochial relief were harshly treated, and subjected to privations unwarranted by the Legislature." The commissioners promptly issued a circular letter setting forth the powers of the bench until the new boards of guardians could be established. But this merely had the effect of opening the entire question of the magistracy's status under the new law, leading the commissioners into "a widely extended correspondence, in answer to solicitations from all parts of the country for more detailed explanations. . . ."[84]

A closer investigation of developments in a single county at this time makes more cogent the commissioners' generalizations about this "ratepayers' revolt." Bedfordshire has been selected for such an examination because its relief expenditure was sufficiently burdensome to concern ratepayers, while its level of magisterial interference had not been so overbearing as to have created an unusual degree of conflict between magistrates and ratepayers.[85] Despite

---

84 For all of above, see <u>First Annual Report</u>, 1835, pp. 4-6.

85 See Appendix B.

this latter consideration, in Bedfordshire, too, the passage of the new law was the signal for overseers and vestries all over the county to review and sharply cut the relief rolls.[86] George Livins, a county magistrate and a director of the Bedford House of Industry, reported that "in many Parishes, the Overseers have already begun to act, on the improved System -- in some indeed rather hastily & indiscreetly. . . ."[87] An even more prominent justice, Lord Charles Russell, wrote to one of the poor law commissioners to complain of the new-found independence of the parochial officers and the consequent threat to the poor: ". . . an opinion has become prevalent amongst them [the overseers], that magistrates have no longer any control over them: this day, sixty paupers of one parish appealed against the overseer on account of insufficiency of relief."[88]

Being subjected to this challenge to their authority because of the ambiguities of their legal status, the Bedfordshire magistrates' immediate apprehension was for the maintenance of social peace in the county. The Amphill Petty Sessions told the commissioners that if the reformed system actually prevented them from ordering outdoor relief, as it was generally supposed it did, "the result anticipated in this Agricultural County bears a most alarming aspect."[89] Urgent pleas for a reassertion of magis-

---

86 See, e.g., Luton Union: William Rudd, Overseer/P.L.C., n.d., c. 24 September 1834, M.H. 12/96; Biggleswade Union: F. Snith, Assistant Overseer/P.L.C., 4 March 1835, M.H. 12/55; Amphill Union: George Smith/P.L.C., 25 September 1834, M.H. 12/1.

87 Bedford Union: George P. Livens/P.L.C., 24 October 1834, M.H. 12/21.

88 Woburn Union: Lord Charles Russell/T.F. Lewis, 21 November 1834, M.H. 12/126.

89 Amphill Union: Amphill Petty Sessions [signed by 5 J.P.s]/P.L.C., 11 September 1834, M.H. 12/1. See also Woburn Union: John Green/P.L.C., 30 September 1834, M.H. 12/126; Amphill Union: Rev. James Beard, J.P./P.L.C., 2 May 1835, M.H. 12/1.

terial authority in relief affairs even came from the all-powerful Russell family in the Woburn district, where they were confronted with a chronic problem of surplus labor. Lord Charles Russell was extremely worried about parochial cuts in relief allotments, because the local magistrates did not feel able "to enforce, or in any way to protect the paupers."[90] Lord Tavistock shared his concern and berated their brother, Lord John Russell, the Home Secretary, for introducing the act into the county with winter approaching and without the proper administrative safeguards for the poor. Tavistock's principal complaint was that the new law had momentarily swept away all higher responsibility in relief administration.[91] Russell at the Home Office reacted immediately by ordering the poor law commissioners to send down one of their assistants, and D.G. Adey was dispatched at once.[92] It seems, however, that this provided little comfort for the frantic landowners, for Adey reported back that he was powerless to amend the situation: ". . . I had a long interview with Lord C. Russell, Col. Seymour and Mr. Bennett, the Duke of Bedford's Steward, on my arrival here [Woburn]. What they sent for an Assist. Commissioner for I can hardly understand. Their questions were more magisterial than poor law questions. Their chief difficulty seemed to be how they were to prevent a congregation of unemployed Labourers."[93]

Adey's comments reveal a startling ignorance

---

[90] Woburn Union: Lord Charles Russell/T.F. Lewis, 21 November 1834, M.H. 12/126.

[91] Bedford Union: Lord Tavistock/Lord John Russell, 10 November 1834, M.H. 12/21. As we have seen, the government had not in fact prematurely introduced the act into Bedfordshire; the overseers had implemented a harsher policy on their own initiative.

[92] Bedford Union: Lord John Russell/Edwin Chadwick, 12 November 1834, M.H. 12/21.

[93] D.G. Adey/P.L.C., 14 November 1834, M.H. 32/5.

of the bench's persistent use of the poor laws to cope with unemployment and thus ensure the security of the social order. What he did not fully understand was that for country gentlemen faced with large numbers of discontented laborers, there was no such distinction between poor-law and magisterial questions. The Bedfordshire landlords had sent for an assistant commissioner precisely because parochial officers throughout the county were extensively, and in many cases effectively, defying the magistrates' accustomed authority in directing relief administration, which had been used to prevent "congregations of unemployed Labourers." The important point here is that the justices -- and as the difficulties of the poor law commissioners make clear, this pertains not only to those in Bedfordshire -- were apparently unable to reassert their supremacy in relief affairs through means of their social and economic influence once their legal authority had been called into question. Under the Old Poor Law, the "traditional legitimacy" of the landowners' authority, so evident in many aspects of country life, was widely converted under the stress of adverse economic conditions into a "rational-legal legitimacy," which relied heavily upon institutional rather than personal sanctions for its potency. The Rev. Anthony Collett, J.P. of Suffolk, touched on this when he told an 1824 select committee that his efforts to compel his own tenants to conduct the relief system in the way that he thought best required "a degree of authority which nothing but the power I am invested with as a magistrate could accomplish."[94] The landlord's domination of county politics and the usual willingness of the tenantry and freeholders to accept the judgement of the proprietors in political matters should not lead us to assume similar acquiescence when landlord power was applied in such a way as to cause the farmers to doubt whether that power was being used in their best interests. Questions which most closely concerned their lives, such as the burden of the rates,

---

94 Report on Labourers' Wages, 1824, p. 57.

could elicit a surprising degree of independence; as the Rev. Joseph Bosworth's tenants in Buckinghamshire bluntly informed him when he suggested a relief scheme not to their liking, "they must attend to their own interests."[95]

Considering the marked and widespread efforts of magistrates in the most distressed areas to provide a guarantee against unrestrained economic interest, there is a strong temptation to conclude that the large landowners were selfless in their administration of the relief system. The reality was far more complicated. One problem arises from the fact that rates were assessed against occupiers of land and premises rather than owners. Since the gentry constituted a rentier class, farming relatively little of their own land, the rates fell much more heavily on other groups, including the gentry's own tenants; thus, the proprietors were among the prime beneficiaries of a pool of cheap labor that the whole community was forced to pay for. This is not to say that the magistrates were entirely immune to the effects of their own relief orders. Prolonged and pronounced increases in the rates often forced them to reduce rents in order to placate their tenants. This, nevertheless, was only an indirect and not always commensurate burden on the large owners.

The thorny question of "close" parishes also muddies the water. Magistrates residing in parishes with little population and few paupers were often protected from the financial responsibilities arising from their relief orders. At the same time, those justices who could rely on the benefits of residence in a "close" parish may have been motivated by a desire to ensure, for the sake of their more substantial tenants, the support of an adequate labor supply at the expense of smaller ratepayers in populous neighboring parishes. All the same, this line of argument should

---

95 Report on the Employment or Relief of Able-Bodied Persons, 1828, p. 40.

not be taken too far. Much the greater part of England's rural parishes could not be easily designated "open" or "close." More importantly, B.A. Holderness has recently shown that such catagories are only of limited use in describing the pattern of settlement in southern and eastern England, the area which saw the greatest magisterial activity. It is also significant that movements in poor law expenditure bore little or no relationship to the prevalence of the system; both "open" and "close" parishes experienced similar increases in the rates in the early-nineteenth century.[96] This suggests that the economic effects of magisterial actions were general rather than limited or entirely one-sided.

Having said all this, it must be stressed that the magistrates' last-ditch stand against desperate ratepayers did not spring merely from the landowners' greater freedom from the rate burden. While the entire community was threatened in some way whenever order broke down, the magistrates were particularly concerned with challenges to authority. The maintenance of order was their special domain as rulers of rural England, and preserving the fabric of deference and ensuring the safety of the hierarchy were far more important to their interests than the economic losses that might or might not accrue from pressure on the rates. The Rev. Philip Hunt was not being hypocritical when he claimed that if he were a small householder, he would be perfectly willing to support the implementation of a labor rate, even though his larger neighbors would reap all of the economic benefits of such a scheme; he was articulating the genuine conviction of his class that the most essential consideration in poor relief administration was ensuring that distress did not become so severe as to threaten the social order.[97]

---

96 B.A. Holderness, "'Open' and 'Close' Parishes in England in the Eighteenth and Nineteenth Centuries," Agricultural History Review, XX (1972), pp. 129, 132, 134, 136, 137-38.

97 Report on Labourers' Wages, 1824, p. 41.

Yet something else was at work here that went beyond the mere safeguarding of class interests. The rhetoric often employed by the gentry to justify and define their relief activities as magistrates constituted an identifiable "morality" that looked to mutuality and social accountability as the proper basis for men's actions. In 1832 justices from all over the country made known to the royal commission their deep indignation at the injustice and "oppression" that ratepayers in vestries were wont to mete out to the poor.[98] Faced with this challenge to the proper ordering of society, which necessarily led on to "the abstraction [sic] of that feeling which used to bind the servant to his master," magistrates voiced their intention to assume their roles as the poor's "guardians," "advocates," and "natural protectors."[99] Some even insisted that such a policy was something more than a matter of prudence, that the poor had a right to protection and maintenance and that the privilege of property conferred an obligation on the landlord to uphold that right.[100]

These articulations of an aristocratic, paternalist ideal should not be dismissed as the empty expressions of privileged men who were only prepared to make mere ritualized gestures toward a justice they admitted. Such slogans prescribed specific modes of behavior and provided clear guidance and sanctions for the magistrates when called upon to "mediate" between the ratepayers and the poor. Crisis conditions, especially,

---

98 See, e.g., Answers to Rural Queries, 1834, XXXIII, pp. 7d, 16d, 100d, 147d, 165d, 198d, 219d, 236d, 241d, 297d, 320d, 338d, 349d, 378d, 396d, 434d, 440d, 460d, 469d, 487d, 548d, 566d.

99 Ibid., pp. 100d, 178d, 253d, 413d, 477d, 586d.

100 See ibid., pp. 165d, 219d. Charles Savill Onley, J.P., of Stisted Hall, Essex, claimed that "this opinion is corroborated by those of many respectable Magistrates with whom I have conversed on the subject." Ibid., p. 187d.

offered ample temptation for the justices to revert to the paternalist ideal, for it was then that the need to reaffirm the older, more stable order became all the more crucial. Certainly an emergency -- and the whole of our period may be seen in such terms -- could be expected to call forth among conservative community leaders a willingness to utilize traditional social institutions like the poor laws in such a way as to preserve the credibility of their rule.[101] Quite apart from the acute problems confronting authority in the south and east, the characteristics of these regions also encouraged greater attachment to older ideals of social responsibility. The comparative dearth of freehold tenure and smallholdings, the small scale of domestic industry, and the prevalence of traditional, nucleated villages in these areas all operated toward the preservation of communities where social ranks were fairly stable and recognizable, and custom well-established and ingrained.

While at some levels of the community the force of custom contributed to heightened appreciation of the role of reciprocal obligations in rural relationships, it was not sufficient alone to counter the encroachments of a changing agrarian order. Conflict between ratepayer and magistrate primarily arose because each had contradictory views on the purposes of poor relief and the imperatives of social and economic life. For rate-paying occupiers and their parochial officers -- mostly tenant farmers and small owners in the rural areas -- the principal priority was to minimize all demands on their limited capital assets. Their central place in a highly-developed market economy ensured that economic rationalization, having one of its chief expressions in a "cult of severity" toward the poor, would shape many of their attitudes to relief administration.[102] This was

---

101 This is not to suggest that they did not believe their own rhetoric. See E.P. Thompson, Whigs and Hunters (New York, 1975), p. 263.

102 Neuman, "Speenhamland in Berkshire," pp. 114-15.

particularly so in southern England after 1813 when the sharp fall in the price of grain sent marginal producers to the wall and increased economic pressures on the survivors. On the other hand, the large landowners, with their greater resources and access to credit, were far more insulated from the vicissitudes of the market. The magistracy, consequently, were not as necessarily or obviously concerned with maximizing profits. For the magistrate, the gentleman, land not only represented income but conferred status, "influence," and a place at the top of the rural hierarchy. And it was this hierarchy and the social accountability that maintained the "chain of connexion" between its ranks that the parsimony of the ratepayers seemed to threaten. The resultant efforts to allay such a threat help to reveal a prevalent feeling among the magistracy as a group that the vestries and parish officers could not be trusted to abstain from pursuing their own "selfish designs" in administering the rates, and that only the bench stood between a harmonious order and "servile war." This in turn created antagonisms that the poor were prepared to take advantage of. When faced with the prospect of declining relief, the laborers never hesitated to play the magistracy off against the ratepayers.[103] Clearly, this situation could be expected to remain tolerable to authority only so long as such an administration of the poor laws retained its credibility as an indispensable counter to social disorder in the countryside.

---

103 Supra, p. 54; Bedford Union: George P. Livens/P.L.C., 24 October 1834, M.H. 12/21; S.G. and E.O.A. Checkland, Introduction, P.L.C. Report of 1834, Pelican edn., p. 37.

IV. Disorder and the Poor Laws

Once the Commission of the Peace had assumed a prominent role in relief administration in southern England, the policy of the bench became a matter of vital concern to those who made it their business to observe and comment on the operation of the poor laws. Indeed, a preoccupation with the effects of magisterial interference colored much of the debate on the poor laws in the pre-reform period. During these years, the method of administration most closely associated with the intervention of the magistrates was the allowance system. This mode of administering poor relief took many different shapes, but they all shared some fundamental characteristics; certainly contemporary articulate opinion tended to see allowance schemes as uniform in essence. The best known example of an allowance system, based on the decisions of the Berkshire justices who met at Speenhamland in 1795, was a bread scale that provided a uniform minimum wage or relief allotment that fluctuated with the price of bread. A bread allowance was computed for each laborer, his wife and children. If the laborer was unemployed or receiving wages below the amount necessary to purchase the minimum bread allowance, the entire amount, or the difference, was made up from the parish rates. Often accompanying such practices were make-work schemes, such as the labor rate or roundsmen system, which involved rotating the unemployed among local farmers according to the rated value of their property.[1]

It was once widely supposed that between 1795 and 1834 the practice of allowances in aid of wages spread to nearly every county in England and Wales, with its chief utilization being centered in the cereal-growing regions of the south and east, the so-called Speenham-

---

[1] Blaug, "The Myth of the Old Poor Law and the Making of the New," pp. 151, 160.

land counties.[2] There are now, however, conflicting opinions as to the actual extent of the system, particularly in the years immediately preceding the reform of the poor laws.[3] The ad hoc, diversified nature of poor law administration in the period before 1834 makes it difficult to determine the prevalence of this method of relief. As a select committee in 1822 noted, the employment of the allowance system "varies very greatly in different parts of England. . . ."[4] The committee might also have added that its use not only varied from region to region, but often did so from year to year and even month to month.[5] Seasonal underemployment, for instance, could spur the use of allowance administration, while it would be unnecessary in the months of heavy labor demands and higher wages. As a result, one prominent authority has recently concluded that until we have much more information on local administration, we cannot be certain how widespread the allowance system was.[6] This, accordingly, is not the place to enter into this aspect of the poor law problem. What is more important here is the nature of the allowance system, its part in the response of community leaders to the crisis of poverty in the countryside, and contemporary perceptions of its effects and range of use.

The occasion for the wide publicity of the Speenhamland plan was the succession of unusually poor har-

---

[2] Webb, English Poor Law History: The Old Poor Law, Pt. I, pp. 180-81, 185.

[3] James Stephen Taylor, "The Mythology of the Old Poor Law," Journal of Economic History, XXIX, 2 (1969), p. 295; Blaug, "The Poor Law Report Reexamined," pp. 229-45; Huzel, "Malthus, the Poor Law, and Population in Early Nineteenth-Century England," p. 444; Marshall, The Old Poor Law, 1795-1834, p. 17; Hobsbawm and Rudé, Captain Swing, p. 75; Poynter, Society and Pauperism, pp. 82-84, 280-81.

[4] Report on Poor Rate Returns, 1822, p. 12.

[5] Huzel, "Malthus, the Poor Law, and Population in Early Nineteenth-Century England," p. 438.

[6] Rose, The English Poor Law, 1780-1930, p. 22.

vests in the 1790s, which contributed to a continuing rise in the price of food.[7] Although an attempt to meet this particular emergency -- and it appears that all such expedients were considered to be only temporary[8] -- allowances were essentially a means of protecting the laboring poor from the more general encroachments of a free labor market.[9] In conditions of a prevailing surplus of labor, wages in a free market were certain to fall behind rising prices, so wages, it seemed, could not be left to the determination of supply and demand, a situation that the interference of allowances was designed to forestall. When so much of the population depended on wages for subsistence, to treat labor as a mere commodity would have been to hand over the security of society to the impersonal mechanism of the market. In utilizing allowances to prevent this, magistrates resorted to a tradition that regarded the payment of adequate wages to be one expression of a community of mutual interests. High prices and the prospect of unrest had long resulted in the subsidization of wages to conform to some local notion of a "just wage," which very often only provided a bare subsistence.[10] The Speenhamland plan, in effect,

---

[7] Marshall, The Old Poor Law, 1795-1834, pp. 14-15; Chambers and Mingay, The Agricultural Revolution, p. 114.

[8] Poynter, Society and Pauperism, pp. 47, 52; Clapham, Economic History of Modern Britain: The Early Railway Age, p. 357.

[9] Karl Polanyi, The Great Transformation (New York, 1944), p. 77; Hobsbawm and Rudé, Captain Swing, pp. 48, 50.

[10] Neuman, "A Suggestion Regarding the Origins of the Speenhamland Plan," p. 317; Chambers, Nottinghamshire in the Eighteenth Century, p. 243; Webb, English Poor Law History: The Old Poor Law, Pt. I, pp. 168, 170, 177; Hampson, The Treatment of Poverty in Cambridgeshire, p. 189. The justices rarely resorted to the direct regulation of wages in the eighteenth century. Hammond, The Village Labourer, p. 133.

merely perpetuated an established custom of fixing earnings according to need and regularized a tradition of differentials based on marital status, numbers of dependents, and so on.[11] In this sense, the allowance system formed part of an economy of provision which was incompatible with economic relations that were devoid of moral imperatives and social obligations.[12]

In terms of administration, the allowance system also satisfied the needs of a landed elite that had not yet fully outgrown a desire to impose strict, personal control over all aspects of community life. The plan firmly rooted poor relief in the parochial structure, with its traditional hierarchy of functionaries operating under the watchful eye of the bench, and, in so doing, severely compromised contemporary efforts to enlarge the basic unit of relief administration.[13] Even more than the law of settlement -- traditionally considered to be "essentially a law for the maintenance of peace and good order, by determining the lawful place of residence for every man"[14] -- allowances, by assuring both laborer and pauper of subsistence, locked a surplus population securely in the local, parochial context and discouraged a dependent population from responding to the intermittent labor requirements of areas outside the community.[15]

---

[11] Thompson, *The Making of the English Working Class*, p. 244.

[12] See Thompson, "The Moral Economy of the English Crowd in the Eighteenth Century," pp. 79-88.

[13] Webb, *English Poor Law History: The Old Poor Law*, Pt. I, p. 266.

[14] *Report of George Coode [to the Poor Law Board] on the Law of Settlement and Removal of the Poor*, P.P., 1851, XXVI, p. 7.

[15] R. Lawton, "Rural Depopulation in Nineteenth Century England," in Mills, *English Rural Communities*, pp. 196, 204; Redford, *Labour Migration in England, 1800-50*, p. 80; Rose, *The English Poor Law, 1780-1930*, p. 28.

Most significantly, the allowance system, in emanating from the bench, placed ultimate control of the administration of aid conspicuously in the hands of the rural leadership. This at once fulfilled their obligations under the imperatives of the deference model, while giving them a visible influence over the means of life of a large segment of the laboring population now that pressures on the poor had increased.[16]

Despite these advantages, the bulk of the criticism of the poor law system in the twenty years before its reform concerned the supplementation of wages from the poor rates. Such a policy could have wide-ranging consequences in circumstances of a redundant labor supply. Since it was the general practice in the south to spread employment among as many agricultural laborers as possible, rather than to confine jobs to the most productive individuals at higher wages, the allowance system threatened eventually to embrace the entire laboring population in those areas where the superfluity placed particularly acute pressure on wage rates.[17] Or so it seemed to many contemporaries. Over a long period of time, observers, witnessing the rise of both population and the rate burden, were convinced that the allowance system was endemic and expanding. As early as 1817, a select committee of the House of Commons concluded that allowances in aid of wages were in common use in the south and that the practice was on the verge of spreading to other parts of the country.[18] In subsequent years, this mode of relief was widely believed to be the norm in the southern agrarian counties; in 1824 and again in 1828, select committees declared allowances "to prevail very generally in several of the southern Counties," the system being "adopted throughout large districts as a general rule. . . ."[19] By far the most authoritative

---

16 Polanyi, The Great Transformation, p. 96.

17 Dunbabin, Rural Discontent in Nineteenth-Century Britain, p. 298.

18 Report on the Poor Laws, 1817, pp. 4, 16.

19 Report on Labourers' Wages, 1824, p. 5; Report

statement of the range and the expansive tendencies of allowances came from the Royal Commission of Inquiry of 1832-34. Even before the commission had been appointed, Nassau Senior declared the use of the system to be spreading daily.[20] This foregone conclusion received forceful support from his chief colleague on the commission, Edwin Chadwick, who pressed this view on all those connected with the investigation.[21] Their efforts and those of other members of the commission who shared similar opinions are enshrined in the commissioners' portrayal of Speenhamland as being "on the whole, steadily and rapidly progressive."[22]

The significance of the commissioners' conclusion was to be found in their insistence that the use of allowances increased distress and undermined the "moral character" of the "lower orders."[23] The credibility of such a notion derived in part from the findings of previous investigations. Virtually all the parliamentary committees that sat after the Napoleonic Wars determined, like the committee of 1817, that "this system is perpetually encouraging and increasing the amount of misery it was designed to alleviate. . . ."[24] It appeared to observers at Westminster that the independent worker was unable to compete with a subsidized pool of surplus labor. As the farmer was already

---

on the Employment or Relief of Able-Bodied Persons, 1828, pp. 5-6. These committees, as well as one in 1833, did, however, note that the allowance system had remained confined to the south. Report on Labourers' Wages, 1824, p. 5; Report on the Employment or Relief of Able-Bodied Persons, 1828, p. 8; Report on Agriculture, 1833, p. vii.

20 Senior, A Letter to Lord Howick on a Legal Provision for the Irish Poor, 1831, p. 28. See also Lord Lansdowne/ Lord Brougham, 25 September 1832, Brougham Papers.

21 Finer, The Life and Times of Sir Edwin Chadwick, p. 47.

22 P.L.C. Report of 1834, Pelican edn., p. 128.

23 See ibid., pp. 155-79.

24 Report on the Poor Laws, 1817, p. 4.

contributing to the poor's subsistence through the rates, he would quite naturally be anxious to receive some labor in return. Consequently, he would economize by discharging independent workers, receiving them back again as parish pensioners, the other ratepayers thereby paying a portion of his labor bill.[25] Not only could the farmer employ pauper labor at reduced wages, but he would give preference to this type of worker. If a laborer had been able to accumulate some property through prudence and thrift, he was ineligible for parish relief, and therefore the local farmers would be reluctant to hire him at full wages. Eventually he would sink into the morass of pauperism, taking his place on the parish rolls, there to receive the same depressed wage as the incorrigibles and idlers.[26] Indolence and imprudence were seen to be rewarded at the expense of industry and thrift, and the line between wages and relief became more and more obscure, the whole system thus tending to undermine independence and ambition, as well as to drive down wages. The laborers faced with a situation that held out few, if any, incentives became, it was thought, demoralized and discontented. The poor law committee of 1817 used the clearest language to indicate the supposed consequences of such a situation for the safety of the social order: " . . . in proportion to the aggregate number of persons who are reduced to . . . unfortunate dependence, must be not only the increase of misery to each individual, but also the moral deterioration of the people, and ultimately, from the concurrent tendency of these evils, the insecurity and danger of the

---

[25] Report on the Poor Laws, 1817, p. 18; Report of the Lords' Committee on the Poor Laws, P.P. (Lords), (101. of 1817), LXXXIV, p. 8; Report on Labourers' Wages, 1824, p. 3; Report on the Employment or Relief of Able-Bodied Persons, 1828, p. 10.

[26] Report on the Poor Laws, 1817, pp. 4, 16; Report on Labourers' Wages, 1824, p. 4; Report on the Employment or Relief of Able-Bodied Persons, 1828, p. 7.

State itself."[27] These, then, were some of the most prominent themes to emerge from the parliamentary investigations of poor law administration: unproductivity of labor, insubordination, and moral degradation of the workers, all the result of a widespread use of allowances.

The capacity of the evils of the system to extend themselves seemed to spring mainly from the effect of the allocation of child allowances in producing a burdensome surplus population, which appeared to stand at the heart of the pauper problem. Since the laborer received an increased weekly allowance for each child he had to support, a correlation between this policy and the marked rise in population in the early-nineteenth century was quickly and easily established. It seemed obvious that the surplus population was encouraged because "men who receive but a small pittance know that they have only to marry, and that pittance will be augmented in proportion to the number of their children."[28] Since there was a redundancy of labor wherever the allowance system prevailed[29] -- most contemporaries neglecting to take the leap of imagination that would have reversed this cause-and-effect relationship -- little investigatory energy was lost in concluding that the excess of population "is in great part to be attributed to the mal-administration of the poor laws during the latter years of the late war."[30] Observers found in the plight of the single laborer an additional factor at work in promoting population growth. As the relief bill was higher for laborers with children, parishioners were thought to be more apt to hire the family man in order to defray the greater cost of his maintenance. Thus, single men were at a disadvantage in the labor market and so were encouraged to marry early and produce a

---

27 Report on the Poor Laws, 1817, p. 12.

28 Report on Labourers' Wages, 1824, p. 4.

29 Report on the Employment or Relief of Able-Bodied Persons, 1828, p. 7.

30 Report on Labourers' Wages, 1824, p. 5.

family.[31] For this reason, the demoralization and acute misery of the single laborer came to be seen as one of the principal characteristics of the allowance system.

By the 1830s, therefore, parliamentary investigations had already done much to establish the need to abolish allowances as an essential step in coping with the subversive effects of poor law administration. Senior's instructions to the assistant poor law commissioners in 1832 pointed unhesitatingly in the direction of abolition, and he continued to prescribe this as the greatest objective of reform in his dealings with the government.[32] Such views supported, rather than induced, similar conclusions already reached by some ministers in the Whig administration which took office in November 1830. Well before the royal commission was appointed, Lord Melbourne, the Home Secretary, declared allowances to be the principal abuse in the distribution of aid to the agricultural laborers. "The great errors which have been committed in the administration of the poor laws," he told one of his correspondents in January 1831, "are the paying of the wages of labour out of the poor rate, and the making a difference between the rates of relief afforded to married and single men in favour of the former. These two mistakes have become, I fear, inveterate throughout the county of Sussex and many of the neighbouring counties, and . . . no system can be safe or wholesome which has not for its object the entire doing away of both these practices."[33] This opinion was seemingly confirmed later in the same month when in a long memorandum to Melbourne, Senior blamed the current administration of the poor laws for "the idleness and improvidence occasioned by making up

---

31 Report on the Employment or Relief of Able-Bodied Persons, 1828, p. 7.

32 Levy, Nassau W. Senior, 1790-1864, p. 86; N.W. Senior/[Lord John Russell?], n.d., c. 1835 (copy), Box #20, Chadwick Papers.

33 Lord Melbourne/T. Sanctuary, 6 January 1831, in Sanders, ed., Lord Melbourne's Papers, p. 127.

wages out of rates."[34] After the publication of the royal commission's report in 1834, the cabinet actually committed itself to the entire prohibition of allowances, agreeing at a meeting on 30 March that the poor bill it was about to introduce should provide for abolition after 1 June 1835.[35] This kind of resolve, however, was too much even for Senior, who became alarmed about the depth of the government's hostility to the allowance system after a conversation with Lord Althorp, the Chancellor of the Exchequer and Leader of the House of Commons.[36] Senior attempted to convince Althorp that it would be more prudent to empower the proposed central authority to make exceptions according to local circumstances and conditions. Flexibility was essential, he urged, in order to avoid the premature disruption of local relief procedures, which "might produce a repetition of the fires and riots of 1830."[37] Even so, Althorp was not responsive to the suggestion, arguing that "unless allowances were, <u>at whatever hazard</u>, got rid of, no real good would be done." In addition, he believed that compromising on the question of allowances would cost them support in Parliament, that this aspect of the bill would be so popular that it would ease the passage of its more unpalatable provisions. He did, nevertheless, agree to consider the matter with Lord Grey, the Prime Minister, and on 4 May Althorp informed Senior that the government had reluctantly decided to accede to his suggestion. Althorp did mention, however, that

---

34 Memo by N.W. Senior, 31 January 1831, Box 35/91, Melbourne Papers.

35 N.W. Senior, "Poor Law Amendment Bill Conferences," n.d., London University Library MS. 173, pp. 59-60.

36 Marian Bowley believes that Senior grew more cautious about alteration of the relief system sometime between 1831 and 1834. <u>Nassau Senior and Classical Economics</u> (London, 1937), pp. 316-17, 322-23.

37 This is a reference to the Captain Swing disturbances of 1830-31.

Grey was also fearful that taking the teeth out of the allowance clause would undermine the bill's support in Parliament.[38]

The subsequent parliamentary career of the poor law amendment bill indicates that the government's confidence in the antipathy of Parliament to the allowance system had not been misplaced. Perhaps the most important factor in the enormous majorities that the bill received was the overwhelming sentiment against the continuance of allowances. A careful examination of the parliamentary debates has shown that condemnation of rates in aid of wages was practically the general opinion in Parliament.[39] For years after the passage of the New Poor Law, the poor law commissioners felt safe in declaring -- and even they went unchallenged on this particular point -- that the legislature's main object in adopting the measure had been the extinction of allowances.[40] Even those who had some very serious qualms about the institutional innovations embodied in the bill, with its suggestion of radical alterations in the structure of poor law administration, often fully accepted the royal commission's strictures on the allowance system.[41] By the third reading of the New Poor Law in the Commons on 1 July, Althorp was so assured of the apparent consensus concerning allowances that he unequivocally announced the govern-

---

[38] For all of the above, see N.W. Senior, "Poor Law Amendment Bill Conferences," n.d., London University Library MS. 173, pp. 83-91. My emphasis.

[39] William C. Lubenow, <u>The Politics of Government Growth</u> (Newton Abbot, Devon), p. 55; see also <u>Hansard</u>, 3rd series, XXIII, 808, 834.

[40] <u>Second Annual Report</u>, 1836, p. 6; Webb, <u>English Poor Law History: The Last Hundred Years</u>, Pt. II, Vol. I, p. 147.

[41] See, e.g., Marquess of Salisbury/Edwin Chadwick, 6 July 1834, Chadwick Papers. Poulett Scrope is perhaps the most obvious example in the Commons of an opponent of the New Poor Law who nevertheless shared the government's distaste for the allowance system.

ment's chief motive in bringing forward the measure. "The object of the Bill," he proclaimed, "[is] to put an end to the allowance-system."[42]

Hostility to the allowance system among lawmakers had not always been so evident. During the Napoleonic Wars, when agriculture was rapidly expanding, there had been little criticism of this mode of relief. But in the post-war crisis of declining grain prices and rising rate burdens, attacks on the relief system became more common among those in authority.[43] The select committee of 1817, the most influential body to investigate the poor laws in the period before the appointment of the royal commission, caused great concern by attributing to the poor laws themselves the deepening poverty of the laborers and the growing demand on the resources of property. "The gradual increase," the committee reported, "which has taken place both in the number of paupers, and in the assessments for their support, can hardly fail to have arisen from causes inherent in the system itself, as it does not appear to have depended entirely upon any temporary or local circumstance."[44] Still, the poor laws remained the main line of defense against wholesale disaffection in a period notable for popular disturbances, the scope and bitterness of the revolt of the agricultural laborers in East Anglia in 1816 producing particular surprise and alarm among the political leaders.[45] Faced with these manifestations of discontent, the government of the period, under the Earl of Liverpool, was always suspicious of attempts to tamper with the ameliorative mechanism of the poor laws, especially as one of the administration's most prominent members, George Canning, firmly believed that the relief system had saved England from revolution during the struggles with America and

---

42 *Hansard*, 3rd series, XXIV, 1055.

43 Webb, *English Poor Law History: The Old Poor Law*, Pt. I, p. 182; Poynter, *Society and Pauperism*, pp. xxiii, 186.

44 *Report on the Poor Laws*, 1817, p. 8.

45 Peacock, *Bread or Blood*, p. 11.

France.[46] If in 1817 reformers hoped for a comprehensive modification of the relief system, Lord Castlereagh, Leader of the House of Commons, quickly quashed such hopes when he announced the government's tentative support for J.C. Curwen's motion to establish a select committee on the poor laws. "However desirable it might be to make some change in the poor laws," Castlereagh told the Commons on 21 February, "the property of the country could not at once escape from this burthen . . . Any notion of precipitate measures directed against the system could not be entertained. . . ."[47] Later, when William Sturges Bourne, chairman of the 1817 committee, moved to reappoint the committee in the following session, Castlereagh reaffirmed the government's continued opposition to any fundamental revision of the relief system.[48]

In the desperate circumstances of the time, however, the government could not rely solely on its authority to keep reform sentiment in check; nor could it afford to appear inactive in the face of obvious distress. As a result, the cabinet was moved to work out a make-shift poor law policy, which included the introduction of a poor employment bill. Unable and unwilling themselves to become directly involved in the administration of relief, the government hoped with this bill to extend employment by making available to private enterprise low-interest credit for the construction of large public works. While the impact of such a policy was bound to be strictly limited, it did represent a genuine attempt to carry on and protect the tradition of make-work schemes for the unemployed and was prompted solely by the "special circumstance of pressure and difficulty."[49] At the

---

[46] Polanyi, The Great Transformation, p. 93; Clapham, An Economic History of Modern Britain: The Early Railway Age, p. 351.

[47] Hansard, XXXV, 524.

[48] Ibid., XXXVII, 154.

[49] Ibid., XXXVI (10 June 1817), 928, 930. See M.W. Flinn, "The Poor Employment Act of 1817," Economic

same time, in the House of Lords, Lord Liverpool moved to establish a select committee on the poor laws in order to counter any drastic recommendations should the more extreme reformers gain the upper-hand in the Commons' committee.[50] This measure bore fruit when the committee in the Lords came down strongly on the side of caution: "Abuses [they reported] have undoubtedly been introduced into the general Administration of the Poor Laws of England; but the Committee are nevertheless decidedly of Opinion, that the general System of those Laws, interwoven as it is with the Habits of the People, ought, in the Consideration of any Measures to be adopted for their melioration and improvement, to be essentially maintained."[51] Liverpool immediately used this report as a pretext to announce that the entire subject required investigation "much more fully and extensively."[52] The upshot was that the Commons' committees were forced to confine their efforts to promoting the permissive vestry acts of 1818 and 1819, and even then the shape of these measures appears to have been subjected in part to government influence.[53]

History Review, Second Series, XIV, 1 (1961), pp. 82-92.

50 Hansard, XXXVI (9 May and 10 July 1817), 298, 1365-66. This was a very real possibility. Both Sturges Bourne and Frankland Lewis, another prominent member of the committee, were openly sympathetic with Malthusian abolitionism. See memo by Edwin Chadwick, c. 1848, Box #20, Chadwick Papers.

51 Report of the Lords Committee to Consider of the Poor Laws, 1817, pp. 6-7.

52 Hansard, XXXVI (10 July 1817), 1365-66.

53 Among other things, the select vestry act provided for the appointment of paid assistant overseers. Castlereagh had actually suggested this reform before the 1817 committee was appointed, and the government's committee in the Lords showed a conspicuous interest in such a provision in their questioning of witnesses. Hansard, XXXV (21 February 1817), 576; Minutes of the Lords Committee Appointed to Consider of the Poor Laws, 1817, passim.

There is some evidence to suggest that the committees would actually have gone further in their recommendations if they had not been confronted with the possibility of government opposition to any more ambitious plans they might have developed.[54] Indeed, the 1817 committee at one point went so far as to claim -- apparently without effect -- that "the House expected at their hands a general revision of the whole system of our Poor Laws. . . ."[55]

It is significant that the government's active resistence to "a general revision" of the poor laws stood in the way of some substantial pressures for reform. The advent of agricultural distress in the post-war period made the burden of taxation one of the chief grievances of the agricultural interest, and with the years 1817-18 seeing the highest aggregate and per-capita expenditure on poor relief in the first half of the nineteenth century, demands for reform became widespread and vehement.[56] This general dissatisfaction was echoed with even greater force in political circles, where spokesmen were able to express disapproval of the relief system by appealing to a body of principles that enjoyed wide and influential support, this period marking "the high point" of Malthusian abolitionism both inside and outside Parliament.[57] Yet the government remained firm in its rejection of

---

[54] See Hansard, XXXVIII (22 May 1818), 895; First Report from the [Commons] Select Committee on the Poor Laws, P.P. (Lords), (62. of 1818), XCI, p. 4; Report on the Poor Laws, 1819, p. 8; Poynter, Society and Pauperism, pp. 286-87.

[55] Report on the Poor Laws, 1817, p. 29.

[56] The Webbs estimate that national relief expenditure for 1818 was £7,871,000, or 13s. 3d. per head of population. English Poor Law History: The Last Hundred Years, Pt. II, Vol. II, p. 1038.

[57] Poynter, Society and Pauperism, pp. 286-87. During the 1820s, the initiative of local reformers largely replaced parliamentary efforts to revise the relief system. See J. D. Marshall, "The Nottinghamshire

"precipitate measures directed against the system" even when allowances may actually have been growing in use.[58] Responsible for the maintenance of order, the government was constrained by a series of conflicting considerations in fashioning a response to the poor law problem in these years of mounting social crisis. In such conditions, Liverpool, Castlereagh, and their colleagues hesitated to tamper with the complex institutions and procedures that had grown up around the efforts of community leaders to restrain and provide for the dispossessed. So to this extent, at least, the provincial administrators and the most prominent part of the political aristocracy were at one in continuing to rely on older techniques of social discipline in the matter of public aid.

On the other hand, one of the most conspicuous features of the passage of the New Poor Law in 1834 was the Whig government's conviction of the need for a far-ranging alteration of poor relief administration. It has previously been shown that by that year Grey and Althorp were reluctant to grant Senior's request for a more flexible approach to the allowance question, despite his instancing the possibilities of future problems for social order, the kind of argument that had weighed heavily with the Liverpool government only seventeen years earlier. To a large extent Senior was himself responsible for the intransigence of Grey and Althorp on the issue of allowances. In 1830, at the height of the agricultural disturbances, Senior had insisted that the mal-administration of the poor laws, particularly the interference of allowances with the proper functioning of the labor market, constituted the primary source of disruption in the rural districts: "The principal cause of the calamities that we are witnessing, has been the disturbance which the poor laws as at present administered in the south of England,

---

Reformers and Their Contribution to the New Poor Law," pp. 382-96.

58 Baugh, "The Cost of Poor Relief in South-East England, 1790-1834," p. 64.

have created in the most extensive and most important of all political relations, the relation between the employer and the labourer."[59] In a long memorandum to Melbourne the following year, Senior outlined a grand program of reform for the government to undertake in order to re-establish social stability in the countryside. He defined the three "great evils" then facing the government to be, first, a partial redundancy of population, second, the mal-administration of the poor laws, and third, inadequate and ill-directed means of education. He believed the first evil, redundancy, to be mainly attributable to the existence of the other two problems and merely advocated emigration as an "immediate remedy." The poor laws, in contrast, presented more complex difficulties and required more drastic measures. The main abuses of the relief system were, he considered, the demoralization of the laborers by making up wages out of the poor rates, the stagnation caused by the settlement laws in preventing the mobility of labor, and the spur given to improvident marriages and population by the bastardy laws. Senior's remedy for the first and most important abuse in the relief system -- an abuse that had resulted in the collapse of social stability in the southern counties -- was as simple as it was sweeping: "That all parochial payments to labourers employed by individuals shall be [declared] illegal."[60]

In advocating such a policy, a policy that Grey and Althorp had come to embrace by 1834, Senior was able to appeal to the findings of a host of parliamentary investigations that for more than ten years had condemned the use of allowances as detrimental to the health of society. So too, his place as one of the Whigs' chief advisers from the inception of their ministry gave his opinions a special significance. But

---

[59] N.W. Senior, Three Lectures on the Rate of Wages . . . [and] the Causes and Remedies of the Present Disturbances, 1830, p. vi. My emphasis.

[60] Memo by N.W. Senior, 31 January 1831, Box 35/91, Melbourne Papers.

most important of all, it was his later role as liaison between the government and the Royal Commission of Inquiry of 1832-34 that provided him with an official platform from which to press privately the notion that there was a direct link between poor law administration and rural upheaval.[61] Predictably, the royal commission's report elaborated his earlier statements and reinforced the government's fears about the state of order in the southern counties, for the riots of 1830-31 are woven through its pages as one of its most disconcerting themes.[62] Still, there is no reason to suppose that this was solely the result of Senior's presence on the commission. Other members of the commission, such as Edwin Chadwick and Alfred Power, were equally convinced that the disturbances were an indication of the demoralization produced by poor law administration, and witnesses appear to have been interviewed with an eye to establishing some such train of causation.[63] The bulk of the commissioners' evidence, moreover, was gathered in 1832 when memories of the riots were still fresh, and it is notorious that the commission's attention was directed almost exclusively to the pauperized, cereal-growing regions of the south, precisely those districts where that very pauperization had contributed to the rise of Captain Swing.

What is particularly striking about the commis-

---

[61] See, e.g., N.W. Senior/Lord Brougham, 7 January 1833, in Levy, Nassau W. Senior, 1790-1864, App. XI, pp. 255-62; N.W. Senior/Lord Lansdowne, 2 March 1834 (copy), N.W. Senior, "Poor Law Amendment Bill Conferences," n.d., London University Library MS. 173, p. 17.

[62] The commissioners actually traced the origins of the riots to the gangs of laborers employed by the parishes in spade husbandry and road work. P.L.C. Report of 1834, Pelican edn., p. 108.

[63] Proof report for Extracts, by Chadwick, Box #18, Chadwick Papers; Hampson, The Treatment of Poverty in Cambridgeshire, p. 219.

sioners' analysis is the degree to which popular traditions of mutuality are depicted as a source of discontent and riot. The isolation of local authorities seemed to have rendered them vulnerable to compulsion, which presented sufficient temptation for the laboring poor to rely heavily on the relief system for support. Because of the custom of making adjustments in the amount of aid according to need, rather than allowing the market to establish income, the problems arising from the increasing pressures on the wages of the laborers could only result in a general demand for more generous relief. The known discretion of local administrators in the distribution of aid -- one of the essential characteristics of a personalized administration of relief -- was thus seen as merely providing "a bounty on intimidation."[64] The most disconcerting aspect of all this, according to the commissioners, was that in those cases where the authorities had not responded in accordance with the laborers' expectations, they had resorted to discriminating violence in order to enforce their supposed rights and the duties of their superiors. "Profuse allowances," the commissioners commented, "excite the most extravagant expectations on the parts of the claimants, who conceive that . . . they are wronged to the extent of whatever falls short of their claims . . . The violence of most of the mobs [in 1830-31] seems to have arisen from an idea that all their privations arose from the cupidity or fraud of those entrusted with the management of the fund provided for the poor."[65] In this regard, the commissioners were able to make great play with the forms of order and disorder inherent in traditions of reciprocity and to show how easily the two could become blurred in the minds of those who were intent on reasserting the social obligations of constituted authority: ". . . the applicant who has been refused relief has frequently recourse to a much more summary

---

[64] P.L.C. Report of 1834, Pelican edn., p. 408.
[65] Ibid., pp. 121, 123.

remedy than the interference of the magistrates. The tribunal which enforces it sits, not at the petty sessions, but at the beershop; -- it compels obedience, not by summons and distress, but by violence and conflagration."[66] The actions depicted here might be seen as part of the efforts of the poor to restore a stable society of interdependence founded upon what Howard Newby calls "the deferential dialectic."[67] But to observers sufficiently removed from the social imperatives of the rural communities, and particularly to those who espoused more "modern" concepts of ideal social organization, such actions and the cultural values that supported them could only appear "anarchical."[68] "The riots, and still more the fires, of 1830," Senior told Lord Brougham, the Lord Chancellor, "were a practical lesson on the rights of the poor and the means of enforcing them, <u>the fruits of which are far from exhausted</u>. That wages are not a matter of contract but a matter of right, that they depend, not on the value of the labourer's services, but on the extent of his wants, or of his expectations . . . all these monstrous and anarchical doctrines were repeated not only by the rioters themselves but by the farmers, the clergy, the magistrates, in short by all the ignorant and timid throughout the country."[69] Thus, both publicly and privately Senior and the commissioners attacked the reciprocal ideals of an older order and never failed to attribute the rural upheavals to the laborers' attempts to secure what they considered to be their legitimate share of the social dividend.

As if to add significance to their findings, the commissioners' analysis of the disturbances did not stop short at 1831. In addition to hammering at the

---

66 <u>Ibid.</u>, p. 182.

67 <u>Supra</u>, p. 27.

68 See <u>infra</u>, pp. 146-47, 149-51.

69 N.W. Senior/Lord Brougham, 14 September 1832, in Levy, <u>Nassau W. Senior, 1790-1864</u>, App. X, p. 249. My emphasis.

theme of the allowance system's role in demoralizing the poor and endangering property with an unsupportable burden on the rates, the commissioners -- just as Senior had done in his 1832 letter to Brougham -- portrayed the upheavals of 1830-31 as a continuing malaise in the countryside, always liable to tear the social fabric again. This supposition was at the heart of their examination of the shrinkage of capital available for agricultural improvements, a problem of special relevance to the pauper question because of the consequent lack of employment opportunities. The dearth of capital, the commission's report declared, was the result of rural society being held to ransom in that the riots had intimidated local poor law administrators and landowners into raising relief and wages. This discouraged holders of capital from venturing their assets in an area where high labor costs and rates were exacted, where an increasingly violent and corrupted work force prevailed, and where a socially unstable situation existed.[70] The conclusion to be drawn from this was that rural England remained outside the control of authority, that the situation had reached the point where it was very nearly beyond retrieve. Indeed, the commissioners claimed that "the most painful and the most formidable portion" of their evidence indicated that the "principal obstacle" in many districts to the improvement of the administration of the poor laws was "the well-founded dread of . . . atrocities."[71] More than anything else, this tone was instrumental in creating the sense of panic that has been seen as rife among the landowning classes after the publication of the extracts of the commission's evidence in 1833.[72] And, of course, the appearance in the follow-

---

70 P.L.C. Report of 1834, Pelican edn., p. 149.

71 Ibid., p. 182.

72 Finer, The Life and Times of Sir Edwin Chadwick, p. 48. Extracts [from the Information Received by His Majesty's Commissioners, as to the Administration and Operation of the Poor Laws] (London, 1837. First published 1833). The Extracts, like the P.L.C.

ing year of the more comprehensive conclusions of the royal commission's report could only have deepened fears about the state of rural society, the heartland of Speenhamland and all that it implied.[73]

Yet in order to explain fully the attitudes of the Whigs to the allowance system in 1834, prime emphasis must be placed on the abiding sense of insecurity that the agricultural riots themselves produced at the highest levels of government. At any time the violation of the well-ordering of society was bound to be viewed with alarm, but what most impressed the government in 1830 was the scale and extent of the rural menace.[74] On coming into power in November, Althorp wrote: "We begin our administration with the whole of the south of England in a state bordering on insurrection."[75] Concern was not confined to the geographical range of the upheavals but, above all, included the objects of the poor's vengeance. A recent listing of the "targets" of the Swing rioters shows that there were at least 80 different incidents involving attacks

---

Report of 1834, asserted that parochial allowances were maintained by intimidation, incendiarism, and violence. See Extracts, p. 3.

[73] More than 10,000 copies of the Extracts were gratuitously distributed to parish authorities and national leaders, while 4,000 to 5,000 copies were sold to the public. The commission's final report in 1834 had an even larger circulation, with 10,000 copies being given away and another 10,000 sold. Edwin Chadwick/Lord Brougham, June 1849 (copy), Chadwick Papers.

[74] On 25 November 1830, an emergency meeting of the Privy Council was held at which, according to Charles Greville, the atmosphere of urgency was unlike any he could remember since the days of the trial of Queen Caroline. Henry Reeve, ed., The Greville Memoirs: A Journal of the Reigns of King George IV and King William IV (London, 1875), II, p. 73.

[75] Quoted in Bovill, English Country Life, 1780-1830, p. 41.

on the gentry.[76] The depth and scope of the apparent animosity toward the rulers of rural society promised to strike at the very roots of social cohesion, and the Whigs seem to have considered such hostility to have been something novel and especially threatening.[77]

To make matters worse, the agrarian upheavals of 1830-31 were only part of a continuing security problem for the Grey government. Besides what was conceived to be the highly dangerous parliamentary reform movement during the period from 1830 to 1832, Melbourne at the Home Office was faced throughout 1833 and 1834 with the activities of the nascent trades unions, and Grey had grown very uneasy about the state of authority in the northern coalfields.[78] Underlying all this was a persistent rural problem, as flareups of trouble, particularly incidents involving incendiarism, continued throughout the first half of the 1830s, only slackening in 1833 before rising again in 1834 and 1835.[79] Just as the royal commission was later to conclude, some in the government firmly believed that the Swing riots had created conditions in the countryside that were incompatible with good

---

[76] Hobsbawm and Rudé, Captain Swing, App. III, pp. 311-58.

[77] Lord Melbourne/Lord Grey, 29 October 1831, Box 41/2, Grey Papers.

[78] Lord Grey/Lord Melbourne, 24 October 1833, Box 5/116, Melbourne Papers; Lord Grey/Lord Brougham, 3 January 1834, Box 8/3, Grey Papers. See also Lord Brougham/Lord Grey, n.d., endorsed: 31 December 1831, and Lord Lansdowne/Lord Brougham, 18 October 1833, Brougham Papers. Melbourne believed combinations to be so inherently disruptive that tranquillity in the manufacturing districts could only be considered temporary. Lord Melbourne/William Hulton, 30 December 1830, in Sanders, ed., Lord Melbourne's Papers, pp. 120-21. In 1831, he informed Grey that "internal affairs are in a very perplexing & alarming state." Lord Melbourne/Lord Grey, 11 June 1831, Box 41/2, Grey Papers.

[79] Hobsbawm and Rudé, Captain Swing, p. 285.

government and discipline. In particular, it was feared that the propensity of local authorities to meet riot with increased wages and relief allotments had had "a permanently bad effect upon the character of the agricultural population" and would gravely compromise the ability of the gentry to govern, laboring **as they were under a regime of extorted concessions.** [80] **Senior, too, may have contributed to these apprehensions.** In January 1831, the same month he was in contact with Melbourne on poor law matters, Senior published his Remarks on Emigration with a Draft of a Bill; in it he argued that agricultural property could not support indefinitely the higher wages wrung from employers by intimidation, and so further disruption must be anticipated: "Sooner or later these promises [of higher wages] must be broken, and the peasantry will rise again -- confident, from having [previously] been successful; and furious from having been deceived."[81]

These problems assumed even greater proportions as the government came to suspect that the instruments of legal repression were on the verge of complete impotency. In an era of widespread discontent, the cabinet watched the magistracy reel before a tide of rioting in Bristol, Birmingham, and the northern counties in 1830 and 1831,[82] while the bench proved so ineffective in the rural districts of the south that

---

80 Lord Melbourne/Duke of Wellington, 10 November 1832, in Sanders, ed., Lord Melbourne's Papers, p. 152.

81 Quoted in Levy, Nassau W. Senior, 1790-1864, p. 70. This opinion was supported by witnesses before a committee of the House of Lords. Minutes of the Select Committee of the House of Lords on the Poor Laws, 1830-1, pp. 23, 47-48.

82 Lord Melbourne/Lord Grey, 31 October 1831, Box 41/2, and Lord Holland/Lord Grey, 2 November 1831, Box 34/2, Grey Papers; Lord Grey/Lord Melbourne, 20 May 1833, Box 5/106, Melbourne Papers; Lord Melbourne/William Hulton, 30 December 1830, Lord Melbourne/Lord Derby, 11 January 1831, and Lord Melbourne/Duke of Northumberland, 21 May 1831, in Sanders, ed., Lord

Melbourne despaired of ever being able to provide for the protection of property in those areas.[83] This kind of anxiety found expression in efforts to establish a professional police force and a stipendiary magistracy, which were among the cabinet's top priorities throughout 1832.[84] All proposed plans, however, ran up against the old problem of finance.[85] This was particularly galling to Melbourne, who felt that taxes were being used to contribute to discord rather than order. "It is melancholly to consider," he wrote to Althorp, "what enormous funds are devoted in this country to the production of Evil, for I cannot consider the Poor Laws

---

Melbourne's Papers, pp. 121-25; endorsement by Melbourne: Lord Lonsdale/Lord Melbourne, 7 June 1831, H.O. 52/13, quoted in A.P. Donajgrodzki, "New Roles for Old: The Northcote-Trevelyan Report and the Clerks of the Home Office, 1822-48," in Gillian Sutherland, ed., Studies in the Growth of Nineteenth-Century Government (London, 1972), p. 88.

83 Lord Melbourne/Lord Grey, 21 December 1831, Box 41/2, Grey Papers. Lord Lansdowne, President of the Council, also saw little prospect of preventing rural incendiarism, declaring it "a hopeless business." Lord Lansdowne/Lord Melbourne, 3 November ?, Box 8/86, Melbourne Papers.

84 Lord Melbourne/Lord Holland, 10 November 1831, Add. MSS. 51558, fo. 59, Holland House Papers (British Library, London); Lord Melbourne/Lord Grey, 17 March 1832, Box 41/2, Same/Same, 31 August 1832, Box 41/3, Lord Grey/Lord Melbourne, n.d., c. September 1832, Box 41/3, and Lord Holland/Lord Grey, 8 November 1832, Box 34/3, Grey Papers.

85 J. Drummond/Lord Brougham, 11 and 20 January 1833, and Lord Brougham, "Explanatory Note sent with the Education Bills & Abstracts to Sir J. [ames] G. [raham], 15 July 1842," MS., Brougham Papers; Lord Melbourne/Lord Howick, 20 July and 19 November 1832, Box 115/1, Lord Melbourne/Lord Grey, 12 September 1832, and Lord Grey/Lord Melbourne, 17 September 1832, Box 41/3, Grey Papers.

as having any other tendency, whilst we are squeezed so close with respect to measures of undoubted advantage and utility."[86] Even so, the government's fears for the safety of rural society went beyond magisterial incompetency and the lack of resources needed to place local law enforcement on a regular footing. By 1831 the ministers were confronted with the possibility that the vulnerability of the magistrates to the demands of the communities over which they presided would induce the bench to deal leniently with those Swing rioters who had been captured. Among the most impressive indications that the government had become doubtful about the capacity or the desire of the magistracy to mete out punishment was the dispatch of special commissioners from London to the southern counties to try some of the rioters.[87] It was these tribunals, under the government's prodding, that delivered the most severe sentences following the disturbances, thereby reasserting the power of the law in opposition to those who were prepared to ascribe some measure of legitimacy to the exactions of the poor.[88]

It is true that challenges to authority in the countryside during this period never achieved the sustained energy and organization of urban-based movements. The demand of the Swing rioters for higher wages and the wholesale destruction of threshing machines, which interfered with winter employment, seemed to show that economic and social, rather than political, motives were behind the disturbances. The government's agents in the southern counties also confirmed this, reporting that the riots were local, apparently spontaneous, and apolitical.[89] Moreover, Melbourne, the minister respon-

---

[86] Lord Melbourne/Lord Althorp, 30 December 1832 (copy), Box 15/92, Melbourne Papers.

[87] Inglis, Poverty and the Industrial Revolution, p. 250.

[88] Bovill, English Country Life, 1780-1830, pp. 40, 43-45; Brock, The Great Reform Act, p. 134.

[89] Hobsbawm and Rudé, Captain Swing, p. 220; Hammond, The Village Labourer, p. 259. See also P.L.C. Report of 1834, Pelican edn., p. 410.

sible for internal order, readily accepted the validity of these reports.[90] Even the king, who was especially prone to imagining conspiracies and to ascribing to the lower classes a desire to subvert order, agreed that political disaffection was not the cause of at least some of the incendiarism.[91] These conclusions, however, in no way provided comfort for the government. The fact of riot on such a vast scale, encompassing as it did entire regions of fielden England, merely underlined the extent to which the landowners had lost their grip on crucial aspects of rural life. Certainly there seemed to have been a general and substantial deterioration in the social relations of the countryside; while distress and disorder had been growing for decades, Swing and its aftermath represented something quite unprecedented, especially in comparison to anything that had been experienced in the eighteenth century. The riots, in brief, seemed proof enough that the resources of the old order, including popular patronage and paternal discipline, were no longer sufficient to ensure the content and obedience that were essential for the maintenance of stability in the strongholds of landed power.

It is remarkable how quickly efforts to explain such a profound disaster should have become focused on the poor law problem. The growing attention devoted to the administration of relief as a factor in the disturbances may be traced in a series of important debates in the House of Lords in 1830. On 18 March, the Duke of Richmond moved for a select committee to inquire into the state of the country and the condition of the working classes. In supporting his argument he used poor relief

---

90 Lord Melbourne/Lord Grey, 11 June 1831, Box 41/2, Grey Papers. I do not find, as does George Rudé, that the authorities (at least those in the government) were inclined to link the Swing disturbances to a wider conspiracy encompassing the political and trades unions. Rudé, "English Rural and Urban Disturbances on the Eve of the First Reform Bill, 1830-1831," p. 99.

91 William IV/Lord Melbourne, 19 March 1831, Melbourne Papers.

returns to show that distress had dramatically increased since 1826. Earl Bathurst, replying for the Wellington government, opposed the motion, at once challenging the relevance and accuracy of Richmond's returns. Bathurst denied that distress existed in the country as a whole, but more pointedly charged that the proposed inquiry was merely a dodge to bring the corn laws and the currency under consideration as causes of distress. He did, however, offer to support an investigation into the operation of the poor laws, using this as a ploy to defuse criticism of more controversial aspects of ministerial policy.[92] In the subsequent protracted and heated debate it is revealing that the relief system was hardly mentioned at all as causing hardship among any segment of the agrarian population, whether landowner, farmer, or laborer. The poor laws simply did not attract attention in the matter of distress on the eve of the rural convulsions, even though a long succession of parliamentary investigations had singled out the relief system as a source of the economic problems of the agricultural interest and the deepening misery of much of the agrarian population.[93] By the end of the year, on the other hand, a noticeable shift in attitudes had taken place. After the Captain Swing disturbances had erupted, the attention of the Lords turned in a decisive way to

---

92 As a counter to complaints of "the Country party" about the national debt and "the criminal profusion of Government," the Wellington ministry held that distress in the country was localized and not general; this position contributed greatly to the unpopularity of the administration, especially after the Swing riots had broken out. See notation in Lord Ellenborough's diary, 25 February 1831, in A. Aspinall, ed., Three Early Nineteenth Century Diaries (London, 1952), p. 59; and D.C. Moore, "The Other Face of Reform," pp. 19-20.

93 See Hansard, 2nd series, XXIII, 476-540. At about the same time, a similar motion by Edward Davenport in the House of Commons also failed to elicit mention of the poor laws in a long debate on distress. Ibid., 391-430.

the plight of the rural laborers. At the same time, questions of government expenditure, the malt tax, parliamentary corruption, and so forth, which had earlier dominated discussions of agricultural distress, gave way to concerns about the allowance system as a source of low wages, declining morality and productivity, and general discontent.[94]

Among the Whigs, anxiety regarding the administration of the poor laws gained ground rapidly after they assumed office in November 1830 and thus became responsible for the maintenance of order in the country. From the start, Lord Holland, the Chancellor of the Duchy of Lancaster, was convinced of the need for immediate and sweeping reform. "[Matters?] in the Southern & Midland counties," he wrote to Grey, "cannot remain as they are, & nothing can cure the evil but a speedy & effectual revision of the poor laws or at least the way of administering them. It is shameful to have deferred it so long."[95] Pressing his point, he told Lord Brougham that "I am satisfied that it is necessary for the future welfare & tranquillity of the country that something should be done [about the poor laws] & I believe it equally essential to the character & credit of the present Government that they should set about doing that something promptly."[96] Similar views appear to have prevailed

---

94 See the exhaustive debate of 9 December 1830 on Lord Wynford's motion for an inquiry into agricultural distress, Hansard, 3rd series, I, 828-95. At Wynford's suggestion, Lord Grey, by then Prime Minister, had agreed earlier to a committee on distress and the poor laws, and while he was willing to allow some license in that investigation, he was determined, like Bathurst before him, that the poor laws should remain the central issue before Parliament. Ibid., 676. See notation in Lord Ellenborough's diary, 29 November 1830, in Aspinall, ed., Three Early Nineteenth Century Diaries, pp. 27-28.

95 Lord Holland/Lord Grey, 26 November 1830, Box 34/2, Grey Papers.

96 Lord Holland/Lord Brougham, 31 December 1830, Brougham Papers.

in the government as a whole. Many of the most important ministers, including Lords Althorp, Melbourne, Brougham, Lansdowne, Goderich, and Holland, considered the depressed state of the poor to stem from population pressure and its effects on wages and employment, and the administration of relief was regarded as having contributed greatly to these conditions.[97] This, clearly, was a matter of serious concern to a government grappling with the social repercussions of widespread distress: Holland informed Brougham that at a meeting on 30 December the cabinet had had an intensive discussion on the poor laws in an attempt to uncover the reasons for "the estrangement which unfortunately prevails between different classes."[98] This, then, is a further indication of the extent to which the poor law question had become linked to efforts to deal with the problems arising from Swing. More significantly, it reveals that from the earliest days of the Grey administration -- even before Senior was well-established as one of its prominent advisers -- the poor laws were at the core of government concerns regarding the spread of social conflict.

There are indications that those actually emersed in the local communities did not generally share the judgements being formulated at Westminster. Eric Hobsbawm and George Rudé have closely examined the replies from the Swing counties to question 53 of the royal commission's rural queries of 1832.[99] The question asked the addressee to assign what in his view was the prime cause of the

---

97 See ibid.; Lord Lansdowne/Lord Grey, 2 January [1831], Box 38/10, Grey Papers; Lord Goderich/Lord Brougham, 28 December 1830, Brougham Papers; Lord Melbourne/T. Sanctuary, 6 January 1831, in Sanders, ed., Lord Melbourne's Papers, p. 127; Hansard, 3rd series, II (22 February 1831), 884; Hammond, The Village Labourer, pp. 322-24.

98 Lord Holland/Lord Brougham, 31 December 1830, Brougham Papers.

99 It now appears that in reaching their conclusions, the commissioners used very little of the information gathered by means of the survey. Blaug, "The Poor Law Report Reexamined," pp. 229-45.

outbreaks. Two things should be borne in mind about the responses to this question: first, the bulk of the queries were answered in 1832 when experience of the riots was still recent, and indeed, when sporadic unrest still continued; and second, the commissioners had managed subtly to word the question in such a way as to suggest a relationship between the poor laws and the disturbances.[100] Despite this, in the 19 counties surveyed, 157 respondents attributed the disturbances to low wages, while 145 named unemployment as the principal source of disruption. On the other hand, only 40 respondents cited the administration of the poor laws as being involved, and even more significantly, only 9 mentioned the plight of single men -- one of the most important popular identifications of the abuses of the allowance system -- as being a contributory factor. In order to place these figures in some kind of perspective, it should be mentioned that 110 respondents considered the riots to have been the result of more quixotic causes, such as the machinations of agitators and conspiratorial gatherings at the beer-shops.[101] It seems likely, therefore, that the government's belief in the relationship between poor law administration and disorder was not based on any hard information being received from the scene of the disturbances. Certainly most local authorities in 1832 failed to see any connection between relief administration and the incidence of unemployment and low wages, the kind of connection that parliamentary critics had insisted on for years.

In some measure this may be a reflection of the fact that the allowance system had probably largely disappeared by 1832.[102] But more than this, criticisms of

---

[100] Edsall, The Anti-Poor Law Movement, p. 17.

[101] The table from which these calculations were made may be found in Hobsbawm and Rudé, Captain Swing, p. 82.

[102] Blaug, "The Poor Law Report Reexamined," p. 231; idem, "The Myth of the Old Poor Law and the Making of the New," pp. 159, 166; Baugh, "The Cost of Poor Relief in South-East England, 1790-1834," p. 64.

the poor relief system were bound to be less vehement among those local authorities who were accustomed to utilizing its administration as part of the arsenal of popular patronage. As we have seen, periods of crisis often served to enhance the value of whatever techniques and institutions lay to hand in the struggle to preserve order. The clash between the divergent "moralities" and priorities of the magistrates and ratepayers in the early-nineteenth century indicates how tenaciously much of the gentry held to the catchphrases and forms of a paternalistic society in dealing with problems of poverty. Responding to communal expectations of support, a good part of the magistracy in southern England chose, for whatever reasons or however reluctantly, to operate firmly within a tradition of legitimizing slogans and procedures.

The government, in contrast, more readily questioned the assumptions that had long supported the social uses of poor relief. Obedience, the touchstone and test of a healthy social order, seemed to have dissolved because the administration of the poor laws produced pauperism and enforced depressed wages, while the obligations incurred by the magistracy in seeking to restore social equilibrium merely raised the expectations of the laboring poor, which the agricultural interest could not economically sustain and which undermined local authority. The willingness of the government to accept the royal commission's extravagant claims concerning the rise of rural pauperism and its threat to the landed property of the realm had its source in the cabinet's deep-seated apprehensions about the foundations of order in rural society. Regardless of the passage of time, the convulsions of 1830-31 and their supposed origins in poor law abuses continued to haunt the Whigs. "I have been occupying [myself]," Lord Lansdowne wrote to Brougham in 1833, "not I trust uselessly in ascertaining the state of the parishes in this part of the country [Wiltshire] in which fires and outrages have occurred. They all bear an exact proportion to the <u>degree</u> of mal administration of the poor law. . . ."[103]

---

[103] Lord Lansdowne/Lord Brougham, 17 December 1833, Brougham Papers.

Relying on these fears, Senior was able, during the discussions with the cabinet on the provisions of the New Poor Law, easily to disarm criticism that the harshness of the proposed measure would produce rural insurrections. He had merely to refer to the seemingly unassailable evidence "attributing the fires and riots of 1830 to poor law mal administration" in order to make his case that the alternative of a continuation of the present system "must be a constant source of discontent and a constant motive to intimidation. . . ."[104] This line of reasoning helps to explain the government's insistence that the unreformed relief system represented one of the chief contemporary threats to order and property.[105] Without question, the royal commission's report of 1834 played a prominent part in linking poor law reform to the issue of social stability, especially in its impact on Parliament and articulate opinion, but such an outlook had long been characteristic of Whig thinking. Certainly by 1831 the cabinet had come to see the poor laws in the context of conflagration and the collapse of social discipline, and this, more than anything else, provided the primary motive, and obstacle, in the Whigs' search for a reform of the relief system.

---

104 N.W. Senior, "Poor Law Amendment Bill Conferences," n.d., London University Library MS. 173, pp. 52-53.

105 See, e.g., Hansard, 3rd series, XXV (21 July 1834), 213, 230.

V. The Search for Reform

By 1830, numerous difficulties confronted any would-be reformer of the poor laws. Among the possible obstacles to reform was the inertia inherent in popular veneration for "ancient" institutions, their evolutionary development being supposed to have ensured that they best suited the country's needs.[1] One of the chief criticisms of opponents of the New Poor Law in 1834 was precisely that it violated constitutional proprieties by subverting the English tradition of local government.[2] All the same, the rash of parliamentary committees that had investigated the poor laws in the years after the war had uniformly condemned the administration of the system, if not its local character, and it is striking how little support was actually attracted to the cry of "the constitution in danger" during the poor law debates of 1834.[3] The poor laws quite clearly shared in what has been seen as a general attenuation of confidence in the country's institutions during the post-Napoleonic period, and veneration for the poor law system had worn thin at least as early as 1830.[4]

A much more substantial hindrance to reform was found in the extraordinary diversity of the relief system, itself a misnomer, providing only a convenient term for the myriad of poor law administrative methods practiced throughout England. It was not even enough to grapple with the abuses arising from the legislative framework subsequently erected on the problematical provisions of the original Tudor poor law legislation. Parliamentary enactments consistently lagged behind actual administra-

---

1 See J.S. Mill, Autobiography (Indianapolis, 1957. First published 1873.), p. 58; E. Halevy, Growth of Philosophic Radicalism (Boston, 1966), p. 81.

2 Lubenow, The Politics of Government Growth, p. 33.

3 The New Poor Law passed its second reading in the House of Commons by 319 votes to 20 on 9 May 1834.

4 Norman Gash, Sir Robert Peel: The Life of Sir Robert Peel After 1830 (London, 1972), p. 1; H.L. Beales, "The New Poor Law," History, XV (1931), p. 321.

tive developments at the parochial level, and there was, consequently, rarely any real connection between the statute book and the way in which local authorities ordered relief.[5] This heterogeneity primarily sprang from the multitude of administrative units in the system. Post-war England was covered with a network of more than 15,000 parishes, each relying on a method of poor relief that in some way, large or small, differed from that of its neighbors. Between 1795 and 1834, over 200 local acts pertaining to poor law administration were introduced in Parliament.[6] Attempts were made in the last decades of the Old Poor Law to enlarge the administrative areas and thus reduce the vast number of units, among the most notable being the establishment of Incorporations of Guardians in East Anglia and Gilbert's Unions throughout the country. By 1834, 924 parishes were operating under the provisions of Gilbert's Act (1782), according them the right to combine with other parishes for the construction of a common workhouse, which was to be used as a refuge for the young, aged, and infirm.[7] In keeping with contemporary views on local control, however, the adoption of the act was left up to the individual parishes, and so the general rule of differing parochial administration prevailed right up to, and in many cases beyond, the passing of the New Poor Law.[8]

An inability to cope with the complexities of the relief system persistently bedeviled parliamentary investigations of the poor laws. This as much as anything else helped to create a climate of despair about the possibilities of reform; Alexander Mundell was not alone in seeing all poor law investigators as having been "as

---

[5] Dorothy Marshall, "The Old Poor Law," in E.M. Carus-Wilson, ed., Essays in Economic History (London, 1962), I, p. 43; Webb, English Poor Law History: The Old Poor Law, Pt. I, p. 149.

[6] Thomas Mackay, Public Relief of the Poor (London, 1901), p. 50.

[7] Webb, English Poor Law History: The Old Poor Law, Pt. I, p. 275.

[8] See Dorothy Marshall, The English Poor in the Eighteenth Century (London, 1926), p. 129.

much bewildered as enlightened by their enquiries."[9] Malthus and others had pointed out the vast social consequences bound up with institutional arrangements for relieving poverty, which gave rise to powerful fears that interfering with such a multifaceted system of relief without a proper knowledge of its operation might eventually only lead to a further augmentation of evils.[10] In 1828, when R.A. Slaney asked whether the government proposed to reform the poor laws, Robert Peel, then the Home Secretary, indicated that the enormity of the problem prevented the cabinet from even considering it. "It [is] in vain," he replied to Slaney, "to call upon Government to pronounce a decided opinion for it [is] impossible for any man who [has] a proper diffidence of his own Judgement to come to one."[11] Nevertheless, Peel was concerned enough to ask Jeremy Bentham, who had done a great deal of work on the subject of poor law reform, for his observations on pauper management, promising to read them "with interest and attention."[12] As late as December 1832, however, Peel wrote in the Quarterly Review that he doubted the possibility of ever coming to grips with the intricate difficulties surrounding pauperism.[13] His

---

[9] Alexander Mundell/Lord Brougham, 20 April 1832, Brougham Papers.

[10] See, e.g., Lord Melbourne/T. Sanctuary, 6 January 1831, in Sanders, ed., Lord Melbourne's Papers, p. 127; Lord Holland/Lord Grey, 12 March 1833, Box 34/4, Grey Papers; memo by Edwin Chadwick, n.d., c. 1848, Box #20, Chadwick Papers; P.L.C. Report of 1834, Pelican edn., p. 206; and Inglis, Poverty and the Industrial Revolution, p. 58.

[11] Quoted in memo by Edwin Chadwick, n.d., Box #25, Chadwick Papers. See also memo or draft speech by Lord John Russell, c. November 1837, P.R.O. 30/22/2F, fos. 202-03, Russell Papers; and Earl Russell, Recollections and Suggestions, 1813-1873 (London, 1875), p. 65.

[12] Sir Robert Peel/Jeremy Bentham, 1 April 1830, Box II(b)/Folder 7, Bentham Papers (University College, London).

[13] Roberts, The Victorian Origins of the British Welfare State, p. 39.

pessimism was shared by the Duke of Wellington, who insisted throughout 1830 that the government could not hope to frame a reform measure. As he told the House of Lords, "the system as far as local practice and arrangements go varies almost in every Parish in England more or less, and I regret it is almost impossible to deal with it successfully."[14]

This diversity in the system may be seen in a positive sense, as an indication of the adaptability of relief administration to the requirements and changing circumstances of the local communities, but it also presented the most awesome aspect of meddling with what had become a highly complex mechanism of social amelioration. In many rural areas, the increasing resort to the relief system as the principal means of shoring up the old "moral economy of provision" had only reinforced the role of the poor laws in defining the customary rights of the humble and the social obligations of authority. Consequently, in the years after Waterloo it seemed to many observers that poor relief had clearly emerged as a key element in molding some of the most critical aspects of social organization. As one correspondent informed Wellington in 1830, "pauperism, which forty or fifty years ago, was scarcely felt, except as to the impotent poor, is now a general system."[15] From this perspective, it appeared evident that in order to deal adequately with a "general system" of pauperism, a general reform measure was requisite, rather than the piecemeal amendment of the laws governing relief that had marked earlier legislative attempts at improvement. But a major revision of the poor laws promised to disrupt a mixed system of relief, which must necessarily compromise its capacity for ensuring social stability. In the end, it was the

---

14 Quoted in a memo by Edwin Chadwick, n.d., Box #25, Chadwick Papers. See also Hansard, 3rd series, I (11 November 1830), 381-82.

15 Quoted in Inglis, Poverty and the Industrial Revolution, pp. 240-41.

social ameliorative function of the system that seemed to stand squarely in the way of any comprehensive treatment of its abuses.

There was assuredly no lack of suggestions for the amendment of the relief system, as may be seen in the innumerable pamphlets on poor law reform published in the 1820s.[16] Even so, because general reconstruction of the system was certain to alter one of the main bonds of social cohesion, all such schemes were bound to encounter serious objections, not to mention confusion arising from the seemingly limitless and contradictory opinions concerning the proper administration of relief. Such a situation virtually guaranteed that reform, if it should ever come, must come from the government, the only authority capable of tapping the sources of information necessary for devising a plan and of marshalling the influence needed to carry it through Parliament and to establish it in the country. This fact was increasingly recognized in Parliament as the impediments to reform became more evident with the increasing use of the relief system in the southern counties. Samuel Whitbread's 1807 bill was the last general measure for the reform of the poor laws presented to Parliament by a private member, and by 1817 speakers in the House of Commons were declaring reform to be a government responsibility.[17] These demands may serve as one indication of growing frustrations with the poor law problem, for this generation of politicians were only just beginning to recognize the legislative function of government in matters that would affect broad features of social life.[18] Yet the cabinet, more directly responsible than Parliament for the maintenance of internal security,

---

16 Beales, "The New Poor Law," p. 312.

17 Hansard, XXXV (21 February 1817), 506-07. See also Hansard, 3rd series, I (9 November 1830), 336; and XV (14 February 1833), 636.

18 Joseph Hamburger, Intellectuals in Politics: John Stuart Mill and the Philosophic Radicals (New Haven, 1965), p. 56; A.V. Dicey, Lectures on the Relation Between Law and Public Opinion in England During the Nineteenth Century (London, 1917), p. 85.

was even more sensitive to proposals that might tend to undermine local institutions that were seen as crucial for social quiescence. These kinds of concerns characterized the poor law policy of the Liverpool government, and only the advent of Swing -- and its apparent connection with the administration of relief -- induced the Whig cabinet to consider the need for revamping the system on a comprehensive scale.

The possible dangers of reform only add significance to the Grey administration's determination to explore ways to alter the relief system. On assuming office in 1830, Grey announced to Parliament that in addition to repressing the rural riots, his new government believed that its first and most urgent duty was to find a remedy for the laborers' distress.[19] His attention was, from the beginning, centered on the poor laws, as in these first few days of his administration he virtually committed the government to their reform, and he appears to have expected to formulate some measure almost immediately.[20] Grey's initial concern, however, seems to have been with the more mundane matter of furnishing employment for redundant laborers, as he asked Brougham to frame a plan for raising subscriptions for this purpose after Parliament had adjourned.[21] Although such a scheme was in no sense incompatible with current relief administration, Grey's request appears to have provided the Lord Chancellor with the opportunity to let his imagination run beyond immediate needs to a consideration of the influence of the poor laws on low wages and surplus labor, a project in which at least some members of the cabinet were anxious to encourage him. "They tell me," Lord Holland wrote to him at the end of 1830, "you have already turned your mind to some

---

19 Hammond, The Village Labourer, p. 320.

20 In acceding to Lord Salisbury's motion of 29 November 1830 for a select committee on the poor laws, Grey specifically reserved the right to bring in a bill prior to the committee making its report. Hansard, 3rd series, I, 690; also see 876-77.

21 Lord Grey/Lord Brougham, 30 December 1830, Box 8/3, Grey Papers.

revision of the poor Laws & especially to that part of them which in practice through the southern Counties has the doubly mischievous effect of keeping down the wages of the industrious unnaturally & augmenting the supply of labourers beyond the demand. It is most fortunate if you have done so."[22] As we have already seen, the riots had convinced the government that the relief system was inadequate to safeguard society, especially since most ministers believed, as Holland obviously did, that the system itself was responsible for much of the distress in the countryside.[23] This perforce raised the necessity of a thorough-going evaluation of future policy on the poor law question. As Lord Tavistock urged his brother, Lord John Russell, "without goading I hope you will soon give us some great measure on the poor laws. Any half-measure wd be contemptible & without something really efficient, the machine must break down."[24]

Brougham seemed especially suited for the task of devising "something really efficient" in the way of a reform measure. He had devoted more time to studying the poor law problem than any other member of the cabinet, and for many years in Parliament he had been a leading critic of the allowance system. Indeed, some of his early associations were with the group of ardent abolitionists who fought with the Liverpool government over poor law policy. Brougham, too, was prominent among those who decried the limited reference of the 1817 select committee on the poor laws, registering his disappointment that the committee had failed to take a "more extensive view" of the remedies available. On 22 May 1818 he promised the Commons that if he could find time from his investigations on charities, he would in the next session present a series of resolutions or a bill for the reform of the poor

---

[22] Lord Holland/Lord Brougham, 31 December 1830, Brougham Papers.

[23] Supra, pp. 108-09.

[24] Lord Tavistock/Lord John Russell, n.d., c. 1830-31, P.R.O. 30/22/1B, Russell Papers.

laws. Although sketchy, the plan he outlined at the time pointed unmistakably to a more stringent administration of relief. His proposal consisted of two main phases: first, "some limits to the progress of the [pauper] burthen" was to be assigned; and second, decisive action was to be taken by "gradually narrowing these limits." He denied, however, that he contemplated simply fixing a limit to the amount of the rates, one of the more popular reform schemes of the period. His chief intention was, he added rather cryptically, "to look to more remote means of operation on the system, by which in time, the same extension of relief as existed at present would no longer be necessary."[25] Although this was some distance from true Malthusian abolitionism, it is obvious that Brougham was not to be deterred from curtailing public aid by the kinds of considerations that induced others to proceed with caution when entering into the subject of poor law reform.[26]

As late as 1834, after the royal commission had explicitly repudiated abolitionism, Brougham was still widely regarded as an ardent Malthusian abolitionist.[27] On the afternoon before Brougham was to speak on the second reading of the Poor Law Amendment Bill in the Lords, Senior found, to his horror, that this reputation was well deserved. In going over Brougham's notes for the speech that he was to give that evening, Senior discovered that they contained "a denunciation of the whole principle of poor laws." He begged Brougham to reconsider his proposed statements, but the Chancellor remained adamant that proper principle required abolition. Even Althorp and Melbourne, who were also alarmed at Brougham's extreme opinions, were unsuccessful in pleading with him on the same day to revise his speech.[28] That evening Brougham specifically

---

25 Hansard, XXXVIII, 894-96. In the event, he never came forward with his proposal.

26 See A. Aspinall, Lord Brougham and the Whig Party (Manchester, 1927), p. 59.

27 Hansard, 3rd series, XXXIII (4 May 1836 [sic]), 591; Poynter, Society and Pauperism, p. 260.

28 N.W. Senior, "Poor Law Amendment Bill Conferences, n.d., London University Library MS. 173, pp. 200-02.

lauded Malthus as one of the greatest "political philosophers" of the age and indulged in an attack on all poor laws as a spur to destructive population growth. Still, he supported the government's bill, confining himself nonetheless to a reluctant admission that public funds should provide for the aged and infirm.[29] Even then, he managed to hint that the bill was merely the first step towards total abolition.[30]

It is not surprising, therefore, that the reform plan Brougham devised in the winter of 1830-31 should have envisaged considerable change in the administration of relief. All the same, before he could persuade the rest of the cabinet to accept his scheme, it had to address a key issue facing all proposals to diminish relief allotments to the able-bodied poor. This was the undeniable, unavoidable fact that large numbers of agricultural laborers were living on the bare margin of subsistence and that poor relief, apparently, played an essential part in maintaining that margin in areas where a redundancy of labor existed. Pressures on the rural poor had become particularly severe in the depressed economic conditions of 1828-30, when unemployment had increased and many local attempts had been made to restrict the distribution of aid.[31] Conditions had deteriorated to such an extent in southern England by early 1830 that Lord Grey and his son, Lord Howick, were unable to account for the way in which the laboring population managed to eke out a living in wages and relief.[32] Grey and his colleagues became even more acutely aware of the extent of distress after they had taken office in November, since they were then confronted with a flood of reports from the

---

29 Hansard, 3rd series, XXV (21 July 1834), 215, 219-20, 222-24. Aspinall, Lord Brougham and the Whig Party, p. 242.

30 Edsall, The Anti-Poor Law Movement, pp. 20-21.

31 Jones, "The Agricultural Labour Market in England, 1793-1872," p. 326; Hobsbawm and Rudé, Captain Swing, p. 91.

32 Lord Howick/Lord Grey, 6 January 1830, and Lord Grey/Lord Howick, 8 January 1830, Box 25/2, Grey Papers.

counties that economic hardship stood behind the spreading challenge to authority. Even after the rioters had forced local leaders to raise wages and relief allotments, the government remained pessimistic about the state of the poor. Lord Lansdowne, for instance, directly attributed the protracted incendiarism in the countryside to the precarious economic conditions of the agricultural laborers. "I am very apprehensive," he wrote to Melbourne, "that wherever wages are abruptly lowered this Turkish mode of redress will be had recourse to. . . ."[33] So too, fears of this sort induced Grey to consult with Brougham on the matter of raising subscriptions for make-work schemes, and Holland, despite his strong desire for a reform of the poor laws, was sensible of the need to ensure the economic welfare of the poor. As he told Grey just days after taking office, "some actual & immediate changes in the condition of the labourers & the amount of their wages, if . . . effected would be a most beneficial measure & I suspect it is absolutely necessary to preserve the tranquility of the Country, for on their present pittance . . . they cannot subsist nor do I in my conscience think they can or ought they to submit to it . . . The question is how."[34]

It is true, as we have seen, that by this time the ministry had come to the conclusion that the poverty of the laborers was in large part attributable to the workings of the relief system itself. But this was taking a long view of the matter. Since any restriction of public aid seemed to constitute, in the immediate conditions of a labor surplus, a threat to the inadequate wages of the rural workers, such a policy appeared certain to encourage continued incidents of a "Turkish mode of redress." Very soon after the ministers committed themselves to the reform of the poor laws, they began to perceive more clearly the implications of their intended actions. "The

---

[33] Lord Lansdowne/Lord Melbourne, 3 November ?, Box 8/86, Melbourne Papers.

[34] Lord Holland/Lord Grey, 24 November 1830, Box 34/2, Grey Papers.

proper relations . . . between landlord tenant & labourer," Lansdowne told Grey, " will never be restored till a temporary vent has been found for superfluous hands, which [would] . . . facilitate reforms of the necessity of which every reasonable person is convinced, but towards which nobody dares at present to take the first step."[35] More than anything else, Lansdowne's comments reveal the full dimensions of the poor law problem for the new government. Although the relief system stood condemned as the grand engine of distress, without the proper safeguards against deprivation, reform of the system apparently involved the risk of resurrecting Captain Swing. The central dilemma, as Holland had earlier argued, was finding a way to provide better conditions for the agricultural laborers without resorting to the poor relief system.

Accordingly, it was essential that Brougham, who was fully aware of his colleagues' anxiety as a result of consultation with Lansdowne, include in his reform proposal a means of forestalling further disruption when the poor came to be subjected to a less profuse administration of relief. Very little is actually known about the measures that Brougham finally offered to the cabinet, but a modest outline of his plan may be reconstructed from scattered references in his correspondence and the occasional remarks he made in the House of Lords. As in 1818, he divided his plan into two parts. The first phase was intended to relieve the population pressure in the south, in accordance with the views of Lansdowne and James Mill, whom Brougham had also brought in for consultation on the matter.[36] In order to effect this, Brougham looked to state-assisted emigration to provide the requisite vent for surplus labor and was very early in touch with Lord Goderich, the Colonial Secretary, in an effort to contrive an emigration project. Goderich agreed that the government might provide some assistance to emigrants upon their first arrival in the colonies so that they

---

35 Lord Lansdowne/Lord Grey, 2 January [1831], Box 38/10, Grey Papers. My emphasis.

36 James Mill/Lord Brougham, 5 February 1831, Brougham Papers.

could more easily get themselves established. This presumably would serve to embolden those at home to risk the hazards of settling in distant lands. The remainder of the correspondence on this subject makes it quite plain that the project under discussion was directly related to a more comprehensive poor law scheme, and that Goderich, too, concurred with his fellow ministers that the population problem had to be dealt with before amendment of the relief system could be undertaken: "I am convinced [Goderich told Brougham] that the removal of 50,000 industrious individuals from the southern Counties of England would cure the evil under which they suffer. The existing redundancy once got rid of, an improved administration of the poor laws would in great [measure] prevent the recurence [sic] of it."[37]

By the middle of 1831, Brougham was in full cry against the relief system proper. He announced to the Lords on 23 June that he was ready to propose a measure for the general reform of the poor laws. He was careful to stipulate, however, that his reform plan was not designed to operate contemporaneously with the emigration scheme; rather, it was to be implemented "somewhat after" emigration had taken its effect, the purpose of the poor law plan being to prevent a recurrence of the surplus population. Brougham, nevertheless, implied that it was only the cabinet that continued to hold his enthusiasm in check, for he declared that he much preferred the second to the first phase of his scheme.[38] As to the shape of the second phase, Brougham was no more explicit at the time than to mention that the removal of the redundant laborers would be followed by "the consolidation and simplification of the existing Acts on the subject

---

[37] Lord Goderich/Lord Brougham, 28 December 1830, Brougham Papers. The policy subsequently received the enthusiastic backing of Brougham's close friend James Losh. James Losh/Lord Brougham, 8 March 1832, in Edward Hughes, ed., The Diaries and Correspondence of James Losh, 1811-1833 (Durham, 1963), II, p. 208. It also conformed to the views of Senior.

[38] Hansard, 3rd series, IV, 264-65.

of the Poor-laws." His correspondence, on the other hand, provides a fuller impression of his intentions. He appears to have visualized a general provision for "putting to labour, the persons maintained at the public expense," thereby directing attention to the question of able-bodied pauperism; there is also a hint here of an appreciation of the deterrent value of relief given under unpleasant circumstances. Most important of all, he had been working out with Lansdowne and Mill a method of increasing the control of the ratepayers over poor relief expenditure through means of "managing vestries," which it was hoped would lead to a more "tolerable management of the parochial fund."[39]

Yet by the time Brougham came forward in June 1831, the main chance had been lost, for the government had already quietly shelved the crucial first step, the emigration plan. In February, Lord Howick, son of the Prime Minister and Goderich's parliamentary under-secretary at the Colonial Office, had produced the opening gambit of the cabinet's strategy in the form of a bill to allow parishes to finance the emigration of paupers on the security of the poor rates. A few months later, another attempt to encourage emigration had been made when a commission of five was established at the Colonial Office to gather and diffuse information on emigration to the British colonies, and later that year the Treasury approved a plan for assisted emigration to Australia to be financed with revenue raised in the colony.[40] Nevertheless, the momentum had gone out of the government's campaign almost from the start. Howick's bill did not receive a second reading before the dissolution of Parliament in April 1831, and in subsequent months no more was heard of it. Admittedly, the bill had been given "a cool reception" by some of the country gentlemen,[41] but it seems that the government itself had come to suspect

---

39 For all of the above, see James Mill/Lord Brougham, 5 February 1831, Brougham Papers.

40 H.J.M. Johnston, British Emigration Policy, 1815-1830 (Oxford, 1972), pp. 163-64.

41 Ibid., pp. 163-64.

its own ability to deal adequately with the poor law problem. In the same month Howick introduced his emigration bill, Althorp tried to halt growing speculations as to what the government intended to do about the poor laws. In supporting Briscoe's bill to increase parochial powers to purchase and let land allotments to the poor, Althorp admitted that the ministry was finding poor law reform "a difficult subject" and urged prudence on the Commons, which was becoming restive, partly as a result of the government's earlier sanguine statements.[42]

This suggests that a serious breach had opened within the government on poor law policy, as Brougham's assertions of 23 June presupposed a continuation of efforts in regard to the emigration bill and explicitly promised stepped-up action on the poor law front. An examination of the context within which Brougham made his statements on the 23rd supports such an interpretation. Demands had continued in Parliament for the government to respond to the desperate conditions in the southern counties. On the 23rd, the Earl of Winchilsea and the Marquess of Salisbury rose in the Lords to charge the ministry with procrastination. Salisbury threatened to move for the reappointment of the previous session's select committee on the poor laws, while Winchilsea announced that he was prepared to introduce a bill to compel parishes to find work for unemployed laborers.[43] To this Goderich could only lamely reply that the government anticipated that its emigration plan, now confined to the emigration commission at the Colonial Office, would relieve some of the pressure on the poor. Lord Melbourne, on the other hand, more clearly indicated that the government was undecided on what course to pursue and, in so doing, revealed his own misgivings about proceeding further with poor law reform. The government, he told the Lords, was in a quandary, since opinions on the poor laws were divided and all previous efforts at reform had proved useless. He concluded with

---

42 Hansard, 3rd series, II (16 February 1831), 607.

43 He had introduced such a measure in the previous session.

an invitation for private members to take up the problem, for "he could not say, that Government had any plan in view on which they placed such confidence as need make any other person, who had any measure to recommend, hesitate to do so." This drew a prompt retort from Brougham in which he maintained that he and the cabinet had agreed upon a reform plan, which he "himself individually" had devised. It was at this point that he sketchily revealed his proposals to the Lords, while his own isolation in the cabinet was perhaps unwittingly underscored by his distinct affirmation of his individual contribution to the ministry's plan. In the event, the government had not been able to avoid the embarrassing spectacle of the Home Secretary and the Lord Chancellor publicly disagreeing on cabinet policy.[44]

A month after Brougham's outburst, Althorp finally and decisively divulged in the Commons that the government proposed to abandon all expectations of undertaking any major alteration of the relief system.

> It would require [he said] a revision of the state of the laws affecting the poor, in order to see whether they could guard against such disastrous consequences [as last year's riots]; but if they look to the state of the Poor-laws, for it was by a careful revision of those laws that some effectual remedy might be devised, it would be found that an amelioration of those laws would, at the present moment, rather increase than diminish the pressure upon the people. He would not say, therefore, that Government were prepared with any such measure, seeing that its effect must be, to increase that pressure which was already felt so heavily.[45]

---

[44] Entire debate in Hansard, 3rd series, IV, 261-67. If we may judge from a notation in Lord Ellenborough's diary, Brougham succeeded in leaving the impression that the government intended to bring forward a poor law amendment bill soon. Aspinall, Three Early Nineteenth Century Diaries, p. 97.

[45] Hansard, 3rd series, V (25 July 1831), 308.

Althorp's statement has been quoted at length because its significance extends beyond the fact that it signaled the defeat of the government in its search for reform. Once again, the paradoxical nature of the poor law problem is highlighted. The government quite clearly remained convinced that the relief system had played a central role in the "disastrous consequences" of 1830 and that reform provided the only hope of establishing a firmer foundation for social stability. But at the same time, circumstances compelled the ministry to admit that tampering with the system would disrupt the economic and social ordering of the local communities, which carried with it the risk of far greater upheavals. Faced with this dilemma, Althorp could only propose, as an alternative, that Parliament vote £1,000,000 in Exchequer bills to be issued as loans to private individuals in order to encourage large public works, such as the construction of roads, bridges, canals, and railways. It was hoped that this would provide some employment for the laborers in the agricultural districts during the approaching winter. This project, according to Althorp, had the advantage of "giving relief, without interfering, in any degree, with the administration of the Poor-laws."[46]

This proposal was a response to obvious and immediate need in a depressed sector of the economy where the workers were believed to be living at or below the subsistence level. Brougham had been unable to convince his colleagues that his plan held out the means to provide a margin of safety for the livelihood of the poor. His course had not been made any easier by the other ministers' abiding fears of his headstrong and independent ways,[47]

---

46 Ibid., 3rd series, V (25 and 26 July 1831), 308-10, 385-86. My emphasis.

47 See Lord Brougham/Lord Holland, n.d., Add. MSS. 51564, fo. 34, Holland House Papers; Lord Grey/Lord Melbourne, n.d., c. September 1832, Box 41/3 and Lord Grey/Lord Brougham, 3 June 1834, Box 8/3, Grey Papers; Lord Melbourne/Lord Brougham, 17 February 1835, in Sanders, ed., Lord Melbourne's Papers, p. 261; and Lord Brougham/Lord Spencer, 18 February 1835, in A. Aspinall, Lord Brougham and the Whig Party, pp. 217-18.

his reputation for Malthusianism, and his expressed preference for a direct assault on the poor laws, the emigration scheme being merely an inconvenient preliminary. His ideas undoubtedly became unacceptable from the moment the emigration bill was dropped. Within these circumstances, the government's options were severely limited, and it is significant that the Whigs, precisely like the Liverpool government fourteen years earlier, moved to counter the prospect of reform with an attempt to subsidize private ventures for the increased employment of the poor. To proceed beyond such a modest proposal would have endangered local ameliorative mechanisms that were seen as undesirable but essential pillars of the social order. In defending the report on his resolution for the issuance of the Exchequer bills, Althorp made it clear that the ministry considered the proposal a necessary measure to maintain equilibrium in those areas that had sustained serious damage to social cohesion. While the country generally was far from being in danger, he said, "it behoved the Government to be provident, to prevent the return of such evils as existed last year. . . ."[48]

Nevertheless, sporadic but widespread outbreaks of incendiarism in the countryside and continued demands in Parliament for the government to respond to the desperate situation of the agricultural laborers increasingly undercut the ministry's retreat from reform. By acknowledging, both publicly and privately, that amendment of the poor laws must form part of any effective remedy for Captain Swing, the cabinet itself had forestalled any possibility that the mere subsidization of private employment would be recognized as the limit of government responsibility in the matter. This was especially so in light of Brougham's uninterrupted efforts to secure support for his defunct reform measure.[49] As long as debate was confined to the cabinet, the government might have reasonably expected to weather the storm, but Brougham's frustrations soon drove him into more extreme courses. In December, he

---

[48] Hansard, 3rd series, V (26 July 1831), 385-86.

[49] Lord Brougham/Lord Grey, 16 December 1831, Brougham Papers.

announced in the House of Lords that he was prepared, as a private member, to introduce legislation if the government did not immediately come forward with a plan for the general reform of the poor laws.[50] Thus, faced with mounting anticipation of decisive action in the Lords,[51] the government could no longer avoid the need to formulate a more comprehensive poor law policy. As Lansdowne remarked to Grey, "in a state of publick anxiety, a Government which does not require legislative assistance [to adopt prepared Government measures], only derives embarassment in meeting Parlt. from the questions & projects even of those who are not its opponents."[52]

This detailed exposition of the events of 1830 and 1831 has been designed, in part, to show the extent to which anxieties concerning the state of rural society and an increasingly serious political problem composed the matrix of considerations which lay behind the appointment of the Royal Commission of Inquiry in February 1832. There have long been gaps in our knowledge about significant aspects of its creation. Historians have suspected for some time, for instance, that some connection existed between the agricultural riots of 1830 and the establishment of the commission but have neglected to explain why the government waited until 1832 to take action.[53] We now know that the resources of the ministry were allowed to exhaust themselves before the thought ever occurred of the need for yet another poor law investigation. Most important of all has been a failure to unravel the reasons for the appointment of the commission and to appreciate the contribution it was expected to make to Whig social policy. It has been widely recognized that the original suggestion for a commission on the poor laws came from

---

50 Hansard, 3rd series, IX (8 December 1831), 130.

51 See William S. Meryweather/Lord Brougham, 27 February 1832, Brougham Papers.

52 Lord Lansdowne/Lord Grey, 21 November 1831, Box 38/10, Grey Papers.

53 See, e.g., Ursula Henriques, "How Cruel Was the Victorian Poor Law?," Historical Journal, XI, 2 (1968), p. 370; Finer, The Life and Times of Sir Edwin Chadwick, pp. 42-43.

Hyde Villiers, an official at the Board of Control, but Brougham has been credited with being the most active promoter of the idea, and if this were so, the establishment of the commission might in some measure be linked to the Malthusian tradition of the post-Napoleonic period.[54] Certainly Brougham kept in close touch with the commission once the investigation was under way, and some of the more avid reformers encouraged him to use his influence with the commissioners.[55] One friend told him that "great things are expected from this Commission, by reason of your having at one time signified it to have been your intention to have taken the correcting the mal-administration of the Poor laws into your own hands. I am therefore anxious that your spirit should be infused into it, in order that this expectation may not be disappointed."[56] The testimony of one of the most influential commissioners also appears to support claims that Brougham had a hand in the creation of the commission. In his history of the poor laws, Thomas Mackay quotes with approval statements made by Senior in an 1841 pamphlet that Brougham "embraced and improved" and "carried out" the idea of a commission on the poor laws, and that he "selected the Central Commissioners," all of which implies that he was a motivating force behind its appointment.[57]

The evidence so far presented in this chapter seems incompatible with such an interpretation. It is not clear

---

54 Levy, Nassau W. Senior, 1790-1864, p. 81; Lubenow, The Politics of Government Growth, p. 32; Finer, The Life and Times of Sir Edwin Chadwick, p. 39; Anon., The History of the Times. "The Thunderer" in the Making, 1785-1841 (London, 1935), p. 293.

55 Levy, Nassau W. Senior, 1790-1864, p. 311; Finer, The Life and Times of Sir Edwin Chadwick, p. 46. See especially the E. Chadwick-D. LeMarchant correspondence in the Chadwick Papers.

56 Alexander Mundell/Lord Brougham, 12 April 1832, Brougham Papers.

57 Quoted in Mackay, A History of the English Poor Law, III, pp. 25-26.

why the cabinet would have allowed Brougham to take a leading role in the decision to appoint a royal commission if he was, in fact, at loggerheads with his colleagues on poor law policy and if his views were seen as intemperate and even dangerous. There seems little possibility that Brougham had reconciled his differences with the other ministers by 1832. Right up to the passage of the New Poor Law, government leaders excluded him from cabinet deliberations on poor law policy, including the cabinet committee established to consider the recommendations of the royal commission.[58] Even his prominent part in piloting the New Poor Law through the Lords was solely the result of Grey's retirement during the poor law debates and Melbourne's preoccupation with forming a new government.[59] Even then, Brougham remained so far out of line with his colleagues' thinking that his major speech in support of the amendment bill ran counter, as Senior recognized, to the main principles upon which it was based.[60] There is, finally, more substantial, less equivocal evidence that Brougham was not responsible for the appointment of the commission. On two occasions in the House of Lords he quite openly admitted that he had opposed the idea, stating that "he was rather against the appointment of the Commissioners, because he wished to legislate upon the subject at once."[61] Mackay himself notes, with some surprise, that Lord Althorp, not Brougham, invited the Bishop of London to head the investigation.[62]

---

58 See Aspinall, Lord Brougham and the Whig Party, p. 241.

59 Lord Grey/Lord Brougham, 8 July and 24 August 1834, Box 8/3, Grey Papers; Lord Brougham/Lord Grey, 22 August 1834, Brougham Papers; N.W. Senior, "Poor Law Amendment Bill Conferences," n.d., London University Library MS. 173, p. 162.

60 Supra, p. 120.

61 Hansard, 3rd series, IX (2 February 1832), 1144, and XV (8 February 1833), 387. It was later that he became a staunch supporter of the commissioners.

62 Mackay, A History of the English Poor Law, III, p. 26.

This suggests that the resort to a royal commission was more in the nature of a response to parliamentary criticism, criticism that Brougham had done much to encourage, than the signal for a full-scale assault on the relief system. In proposing a poor law investigation, Hyde Villiers specifically mentioned the need to satisfy expectations excited by the government's public promises of reform.[63] It has already been shown, moreover, that from at least the middle of 1831 the cabinet had directed its efforts more and more to avoiding the issue and withstanding pressures to interfere with the relief system. This was especially true in the case of Lord Melbourne, who had grown increasingly cautious as the possibility of comprehensive reform loomed larger. Early in 1831 he approved a plan to establish committees of gentlemen in each county to institute enquiries into the state of parochial administration, although he did caution that "such an inquiry and such measures [as would be suggested] must be conducted on sound and enlightened principles, or they may aggravate the evils instead of removing them."[64] Only six months later, however, he was denying any intention on the part of the government to produce a general reform of the relief system.[65] This "retreat from reform" appears to have carried the government through the remainder of the year, as it is notable that the King's Speech on 6 December 1831 opening the 1831-32 session of Parliament scrupulously avoided mention of the poor laws, only two months before the appointment of the royal commission.

In line with its establishment as an ad hoc, stop-gap project, in its early stages the royal commission was seen as having only a circumscribed role in the formulation of government policy. Government expectations of results were not high. Looking back in 1834, Althorp conceded that at the time of its appointment he

---

63 Ibid., p. 26.

64 Lord Melbourne/T. Sanctuary, 6 January 1831, in Sanders, ed., Lord Melbourne's Papers, p. 127.

65 Hansard, 3rd series, IV (24 June 1831), 284-85.

had not thought the commission would be able to accomplish more than demonstrate, like other investigations before it, that in some parishes the administration of the poor laws was beneficial, while in others it was riddled with abuses.[66] This pessimism was strengthened by forebodings that the commission, too, would eventually prove to be a dangerous expedient. When informing the Commons of the commission's appointment, Althorp attempted to dispel any notion that the government had relented in its resistance to the general reform of the poor laws. The subject of reform, he insisted, was of "such great magnitude, and involved such a variety of important considerations" that efforts must be confined to the amendment of only limited portions of the relief system.[67] These modest aspirations were obviously in opposition to those of fervent reformers such as Brougham, which once again led to divisions in the cabinet. While Althorp continued to maintain that the commission had a restricted mandate and would consequently complete its work in only a short time, Brougham was equally insistent, once the government had committed itself to an investigation, that the commission would provide the basis for a sweeping reform and so would require more time to report.[68]

In only a limited sense, then, did the appointment of the royal commission mark a turning point in ministerial thinking. As late as 1832, the cabinet continued to drift, apparently trapped into taking action that seemed likely to compound the difficulties of government. In Parliament, too, the distress and discontent of the agricultural workers continued to stir a desire for some change in the condition of labor, a change, however, which ultimately seemed beyond the capacity of legislators to effect. The measures suggested and adopted in this period were generally temporary expedients, neglecting completely to treat the deeper causes of rural

---

66 Ibid., XXII (17 April 1834), 876.

67 Ibid., IX (1 February 1832), 1099.

68 Ibid., IX (1 and 3 February 1832), 1099, 1233-34; extract by Edwin Chadwick, n.d., Box #22, Chadwick Papers.

poverty. This, in conjunction with the indecisiveness of the government on a matter of critical importance, provided the royal commission with a unique opportunity to influence the eventual solution of the poor law problem.

Beginning in 1831, and continuing up to 1834, a considerable number of schemes pertaining to the relief system were presented to Parliament. While the necessity for some kind of palliative was recognized in the Commons, activity was especially brisk in the Lords, where bills were introduced by the Duke of Richmond, the Earl of Winchilsea, and Lords Teynham, Nugent, and Kenyon. In 1831 and 1832 three acts (1 and 2 William IV, c. 42 and c. 59, and 2 William IV, c. 42) were adopted that allowed parochial authorities to enclose wastes, commons, and Crown lands for the purpose of letting allotments to the laborers.[69] These were followed in 1832 by an act "for the better employment of laborers in agricultural parishes," which provided for the wider use of the labor rate system.[70] As always, these measures and others like them met with conflicting opinions about the proper course to pursue with respect to poor law administration, but the purpose of the bills that actually reached the statute book in these years is clear. They were concerned with providing relief for a palpable and urgent need through increased parochial employment and the extension of parochial aid in the form of leases on small gardens.

This suggests that Parliament was generally disinclined to constrict aid or substantially alter the relief system, at least while the rural areas remained in turmoil. The shock of the riots plainly had their effect on the shape of parliamentary relief measures. In the country at large, the number of pamphlets, periodicals, and articles advocating allotment schemes greatly increased after 1830,

---

69 For the provisions of these acts, see Webb, English Poor Law History: The Old Poor Law, Pt. I, p. 230.

70 For the provisions of this act (2 & 3 William IV, c. 96), see Nicholls, A History of the English Poor Law, II, pp. 214-15.

and this has been linked to the reaction to rural unrest.[71] As the 1843 select committee on allotments noted, "it was not until 1830, when discontent had been so painfully exhibited amongst the peasantry of the southern counties, that this method of alleviating their situation [i.e., allotments] was much resorted to."[72] During the debates on the various proposals for dealing with the pauper problem, reference was often made to the necessity of avoiding "the recurrence of those outrages and that system of terror which, in the Autumn of 1830, disgraced the fairest portion of England."[73] The manifest concern was for a return to some kind of normalcy through the protection of the poor's subsistence, or by means of even grander objects, such as Lord Kenyon's Agricultural Labourers' Employment Bill, which was intended to provide land for the laborers from commons and wastes in order to put them "upon the footing of small farmers."[74]

The tendency towards this sort of legislation may be discerned from the last months of the Wellington administration, when the existence of widespread distress could no longer be ignored. The parliamentary clamor that Wellington had to deal with in regard to the poor concerned, for the most part, the question of whether or not his government planned to introduce measures for extended relief to the stricken laborers.[75] The tenor of

---

71 Barnett, "Allotments and the Problem of Rural Poverty, 1780-1840," pp. 174-75; G.E. Fussell, From Tolpuddle to T.U.C.: A Century of Farm Labourers' Politics (Slough, 1948), p. 40.

72 Report on Labouring Poor (Allotments of Land), 1843, p. iii. See also, Jones, "The Agricultural Labour Market in England, 1793-1872," p. 330; and Hammond, The Village Labourer, pp. 160-61.

73 The Duke of Richmond on the second reading of his labor rate bill, Hansard, 3rd series, XVIII (13 June 1833), 678-79. See also, e.g., ibid., IV (23 June 1831), 263; VI (22 August 1831), 379-80; XXIII (30 April 1834), 308.

74 Ibid., 3rd series, XI (13 March 1832), 126-28.

75 See Hansard, 2nd series, XXIII (18 March 1830), 476-85; 3rd series, I (9 November 1830), 334-38.

the Lords' committee on the poor laws which sat in November and December of 1830 presents a good illustration of the prevailing mood at this time. The questions put to witnesses before the committee differed markedly from those of previous committee investigations of the relief system. There was a more concentrated effort to ascertain the economic state of agriculture and the condition of the laborers, as may be seen in the numerous questions regarding wages, piece rates, employment opportunities, cost of provisions and clothing, cottage rent, habits of consumption, and so forth. Concern with these issues was so intense, in fact, that the poor laws themselves had a tendency to slip from consideration, except insofar as they were portrayed as being crucial to the survival of the poor. It is particularly noticeable that there was less inquiry as to the modes of administration and the effects of misapplied relief than had been evident in previous investigations, the committee members' principal concern centering on whether or not the relief system provided sufficient support.[76] So too, the 1830 committee appears to have been less inclined to attack the poor laws, even though belief in their subversive aspects was already widespread in the Lords. This point is reflected in the fact that in two reports of only two pages each, the committee refrained from making any recommendations regarding the administration of relief.

If the nervousness of 1830 and the acts of 1831-32 may be regarded as characteristic of the predominant temper in Parliament, it is unlikely that Brougham's plan for more stringent relief administration could ever have made its way without staunch government support; indeed, even the initial phase was not well received. What the government dreaded was that Brougham's ideas might prove politically damaging if he should succeed in tapping the vein of abolitionism and hostility to the relief system that was still extant and potent, especially in the Commons. Without Brougham's decisiveness, on the other

---

76 See Minutes of Evidence of the Select Committee of the House of Lords Appointed to Consider of the Poor Laws, 1830-1, passim.

hand, the government remained at sea on poor law matters, the more so as it became clear that the royal commission could not be relied upon to come quickly to even a partial solution to the pauper problem. Lansdowne told Brougham seven months after the appointment of the commissioners that "I am more than ever satisfied that another Session cannot pass without applying some corrective (remedy I am assured is hopeless) to an evil which is threatening at once the rental of the landlord, the wages & character of the laborer, & the peace of the country." Yet all that he could suggest as a corrective was an alteration of the laws of settlement and "a rigid system of scrutiny into parochial accounts. . . ."[77] More than a year later he was even less sure of his ground, although the commission by that time had come to hold out some prospect of salvation: "[Lord] Radnor writes to me in great alarm at the prevailing spirit amongst the labouring classes in parts of the Country, which being in constant attendance at Sessions etc., etc. he has good opportunities of observing. He points however at no remedy, & untill [sic] we see what can be done upon the report of the poor law Commissioners, I know of none. . . ."[78] In these same years we find Melbourne at the Home Office listlessly encouraging friends of the king to proceed with experiments in road construction for the purpose of creating more jobs, and Althorp worrying about the state of the benefit societies.[79] Some other members of the government were drawn into promoting more utopian schemes, such as Lord Holland and Lord John Russell, who supported the National Society for the Employment and Education of the Poor, which proposed to raise capital to set poor boys to work, the profits going to pay for their maintenance and education. The basis of the

---

77 Lord Lansdowne/Lord Brougham, 25 September 1832, Brougham Papers.

78 Lord Lansdowne/Lord Grey, 11 December 1833, Box 38/10, Grey Papers.

79 Sir Herbert Taylor/Lord Melbourne, 28 December 1830, and Lord Melbourne/Sir Herbert Taylor, 14 January 1831 (copy), Lord Althorp/Lord Melbourne, n.d., c. 12 November 1831, Box 15/90, Melbourne Papers.

plan, one reflecting current concerns but also indicating its futility, was that the boys were to be trained in agricultural pursuits.[80] Even the Postmaster General, the Duke of Richmond, who was so prominent as an individual in bringing forward allotment and labor rate bills, did not believe that his measures would have much impact on the pauper problem, and all that Lansdowne could find to say about one of Richmond's allotment bills was that "it will tend to give satisfaction, & there is such a desire to get something done, that it is fortunate when a something can be found that is innocent."[81]

In view of such uncertainty, it is not surprising that the government gradually relinquished leadership on poor law policy. The chief reforms of the period were introduced by private members, or in the case of Richmond, a minister acting as an individual. The government was content to give its support to several of these bills, including Briscoe's plan to increase the acreage that parishes were authorized to purchase or lease for providing employment for the poor, Weyland's allotment bill, and the Duke of Richmond's labor rate bill of 1833.[82] The significance of the government's reaction to these proposals is that it shows that the ministry was receptive to measures that called for the extension of relief and that it was not this element of the reform movement in Parliament that it hoped to divert. In effect, by the middle of 1831 parliamentary policy was fast becoming government policy.

It has recently been argued that both the government and Parliament did not, in fact, regard the rural disturbances of 1830-31 as of great importance or as a

---

[80] William Sturges Bourne/Lord Melbourne, 4 February 1831 (enclosure), Box 20/1, 1A, Melbourne Papers. Holland was anxious that Melbourne, too, support this project.

[81] Lord Lansdowne/Lord Melbourne, n.d., Box 8/78, Melbourne Papers.

[82] Hansard, 3rd series, II (16 February 1831), 606-07; XI (15 March 1832), 286-90; XVIII (13 June 1833), 664-79. The government had earlier opposed a labor rate measure introduced by the Earl of Winchilsea in 1831. Ibid., IV (7 July 1831), 930-42.

real threat to social stability.[83] This judgement is based on the trifling provisions of and the mixed reception given to the measures that were designed in these years to provide relief for the agricultural laborers. This argument, however, ignores the feelings of hopelessness regarding the value of legislation in combating distress, which were only strengthened as the search for poor law reform advanced. In other respects, the disturbances succeeded in launching a major government attempt at the formulation of a poor law policy and in actuating an impatient spirit in Parliament for the mitigation of distress. The two allotment acts of 1831, for instance, were rushed through Parliament in the extraordinarily short time of three and four days.[84] Politicians, both in the cabinet and Parliament, believed the relief system to be a factor in the demoralization of the laborers and the deterioration of their earning power, but would-be reformers were prevented from dealing with these destructive elements by apprehensions of a "Turkish mode of redress" in the countryside. Thus, it was <u>because</u> the politicians -- and this particularly applies to the cabinet -- were so concerned about the implications of the rural riots that their relief measures now appear paltry; they were faced with the frightening possibility that their cures might prove more dangerous than the disease.

Westminster's dilemma was not entirely unlike that facing local authorities in the years leading up to 1830. The distribution of public aid had become such an accepted part of the protections accorded the subsistence of the poor that the administration of relief constituted the ultimate test of the rulers' goodwill in supporting popular expectations and ideals. This was no small matter in a society that to a considerable extent still relied on the rituals of authority and popular patronage as a source of stability. For this reason, in part, the parliamentary measures of 1831-32 had a distinctly traditional flavor.

---

[83] Dunbabin, <u>Rural Discontent in Nineteenth-Century Britain</u>, pp. 299-300.

[84] Barnett, "Allotments and the Problem of Rural Poverty, 1780-1840," pp. 179-80.

The labor rate had long been an accepted practice of providing employment for superfluous hands, and the institutionalization of underemployment was grounded on the right of local authorities to interfere with the workings of the labor market. Allotment schemes, too, had already achieved a solid place in the history of paternalism, their use dating back to the end of the eighteenth century and finding strong support among such great landowners as the Duke of Ancaster, the Earl of Winchilsea, and Lords Carrington and Suffield. In the words of the historian of the allotment movement, "this was less a programme of social progress than a backward-looking appeal to a golden age of a landholding peasantry, a fairly typical reaction of a conservative section of rural society in an age of profound social change."[85]

This reluctance to part with the instruments and techniques of paternal control in the aftermath of Swing proved, in the event, to be short-lived. John Weyland's allotment act of June 1832 was the last of such legislation. A select committee of the Commons reported against the use of the labor rate in August 1833.[86] The Lords' labor rate bill of that year failed to pass the Commons, and a similar bill introduced by Sir Charles Burrell was also defeated in the same year despite the government's support for it as a temporary measure.[87] To some extent this reflects the gathering strength in the Commons of traditional objections to practices that were seen as intrinsically detrimental to society. Even so, 1833 appears to mark a genuine change in attitudes to public aid among a wider range of politicians than those who had long voiced hostility to the relief system. Certainly the hardening outlook that may be detected in that year is in contrast to the general tenor of the legislation

---

85 Ibid., pp. 171-72.

86 Report on Agriculture, 1833, p. vii.

87 Hansard, 3rd series, XX (5 August 1833), 357. Burrell introduced a similar bill in the following year, but this time Althorp opposed it because "now an efficient remedy was introduced. . .," i.e., the Poor Law Amendment Bill. Ibid., XXIV (4 June 1834), 154.

of 1831-32.

In no sense was this change the result of fading memories of the rural riots, since a continuation of anonymous violence kept alive a sense of urgency about the disposition of surplus labor. At the same time, the publication in 1833 of the royal commission's _Extracts_ of evidence helped to sustain apprehensions about the progressive deterioration of cohesion and social organization in the rural areas. This provided the commission with a highly favorable environment in which to "educate" political opinion on the pitfalls of continuing to rely on traditional approaches to the problem of poverty; certainly the commissioners' influence was beginning to be felt by 1833. In addition to the appearance of _Extracts_, in that same year the commissioners came out strongly against labor rate schemes.[88] Friends of the commissioners were extremely active in publicizing their views and worked in Parliament to frustrate efforts to pass the labor rate bill of 1833, with the Bishop of London, the head of the commission, leading the opposition in the Lords.[89] By 1833, the commission had in effect become an independent authority on the poor laws, opposing even government-supported legislation.

It is true that the ideas of the royal commission grew out of a decades-old tradition of debate and that criticism of the relief system, particularly the use of allowances, had become part of the intellectual small change of the period. Nevertheless, as J.R. Poynter insists, the commission's work must be seen as an interruption, rather than a continuation, of past efforts to deal with the questions of poverty and authority's proper relationship to the poor.[90] The "principles of 1834" not

---

88 _Copy of the Letter Addressed by the Chancellor of the Exchequer to the Poor Law Commissioners . . . and of the Answer Returned by the Commissioners_, P.P. (Lords), (71. of 1833), CCCXXIV, pp. 2-4.

89 Webb, _English Poor Law History: The Old Poor Law_, Pt. I, pp. 195-96; Finer, _The Life and Times of Sir Edwin Chadwick_, p. 98.

90 _Society and Pauperism_, p. 300. It is significant that the commissioners devoted special sections of their

only provided a final answer to the demands of abolitionism; they also differed in kind, as well as degree, from the methods that had characterized parliamentary tinkering with the relief system in the years leading up to 1833. Undaunted by the vast complexity of current provisions for public aid, the royal commission argued for the systematic application of universal sanctions to combat pauperism, which, if fully implemented, promised to subvert an "ancient" method of government. To a considerable extent, the appeal of this argument may be attributed to a paralysis of political leadership in the face of a continuing social crisis, for in the end there seemed few alternatives to the vision of poverty and the poor that the royal commission offered England's rulers.

---

report to arguing specifically against the use of labor rates and the public support of allotment schemes. See <u>P.L.C. Report of 1834</u>, Pelican edn., pp. 278-94, 294-333.

VI. Conclusion

From at least the end of the Napoleonic Wars, many of the political aristocracy regarded the administration of the relief system as a threat to property and an element of potential disruption in rural society. The formulation of these concepts largely resulted from a need to explain the steady advance of expenditure on relief during a period of increasing economic hardship for the poor. In 1801 annual relief expenditure was £3,750,000; by 1818 it had reached £7,871,000, an increase of more than 100 percent.[1] After this high-tide mark, however, expenditure declined and remained somewhat steady for more than a decade, a situation reflected in the lack of serious plans to alter the main outlines of the poor laws during the 1820s.[2] Reinforcing this reluctant but effective acquiescence in the operation of the relief system was the determination of the Tory ministries of the period (Liverpool's and Wellington's) to resist change in an institution that was regarded as an essential component of a society bound in some measure by the conventions of customary authority.

With the publication of the royal commission's report in 1834, this resistance to reform, already severely weakened by the shocks of Captain Swing, collapsed across a wide front of governmental and parliamentary opinion. In part, this was the result of the commissioners' effectiveness in criticizing the current administration of relief. All the old accusations were rehearsed with great conviction and extensive elaboration: allowances demoralized labor, drove down wages, increased population, undercut production, inflated rates, encouraged discontent. This alone, however, was not sufficient to compel the degree of change in administration that the commission recommended, as Brougham had found to his considerable frustration only two years earlier. The

---

1 Webb, English Poor Law History: The Last Hundred Years, Pt. II, Vol. II, pp. 1037-38.

2 Annual relief expenditure in 1830 amounted to £6,829,000. Ibid., p. 1038.

commissioners' vital contribution to the solution of the poor law problem rested instead in their determination to break with the Malthusian tradition of abolitionism and to propagate an alternative theoretical basis for reform.

While the commissioners accepted many elements of the Malthusian analysis of poverty, they rejected its claims of universality. They took the position that only in circumstances of declining productivity was the Malthusian process engaged, that the pressures of rising population on the condition of the laboring poor could be successfully counteracted by increasing worker productivity.[3] If laborers were more steady and diligent, their greater efficiency would augment employers' profits, which in turn would create a larger fund from which to pay higher wages.[4] At the same time, employers would be more anxious to hire industrious, i.e., profitable, workers, increasing the general demand for labor. In order to give life to this process of escalating wages and labor demands, it was first necessary to breakup the allowance system, to force pauper labor back onto the open market, where the dynamics of competition for employment would encourage greater labor efficiency. This did not require the formal abolition of the right of the poor to public aid; rather, administration of relief could be cast in such a way as to provide for genuine need without corrupting the laboring population. Scattered experiments in the use of well-regulated workhouses as deterrent mechanisms had, it was claimed, produced a significant transformation in the behavior and condition of agricultural laborers:

> 1. Their industry has been restored and improved.
> 2. Frugal habits have been created or

---

[3] Memo by Edwin Chadwick, n.d., Box #85 and _idem_, "Notes on Preparation for Legislation," n.d., Box #81, Chadwick Papers; Finer, _The Life and Times of Edwin Chadwick_, pp. 25-26, 44-48.

[4] _P.L.C. Report of 1834_, Pelican edn., pp. 348-49.

strengthened.

3. The permanent demand for their labour has increased.
4. And the increase has been such, that their wages, so far from being depressed by the increased amount of labour in the market, have in general advanced.
5. The number of improvident and wretched marriages has diminished.
6. Their discontent has been abated, and their moral and social condition in every way improved.[5]

Here, then, in the commissioners' own simple summation was the crux of their argument for the re-direction of relief administration and the general use of workhouses to discourage applications to the parishes for aid. It was, ultimately, an argument designed to support efforts to institutionalize on a grand scale the conviction that a relief system should contribute as far as possible to the preservation of a fully competitive labor market.

The probability that such a scheme would effect authentic social change did not detract from its appeal, for the pauper problem seemed to go deeper than questions of poor law administration <u>per se</u>. "The views . . . on which [the New Poor Law] was proposed," Edwin Chadwick insisted, "went beyond measures of cure or alleviation or the repression of evil to prevention and by preventive measures to the improvement of the condition of the population."[6] Although English rural society in the early-nineteenth century may not be properly characterized as paternal, it has been shown to what extent the royal commission's criticism of poor law administration assumed that the values of a paternal society sustained the operation of the allowance system. Paternalism -- with its main emphasis on the manipulation of fear and gratitude for the legitimization of personal authority and

---

[5] <u>Ibid.</u>, p. 374.

[6] Memo: "Poor Law Notes on its Offshoots: Sanitary," n.d., Box #25, Chadwick Papers.

prestige -- appeared to have failed to maintain a healthy social order because it had been unable to raise the laborers' condition, both morally and economically. Too much energy had been directed to assuring a reconciliation to the _status quo_ through a mere stabilization of conditions or a reversion to traditional protective devices, which bound labor to the dead weight of custom and the interests of local elites. For some supporters of the New Poor Law in Parliament this seemed to have led to "a state of absolute slavery" in which poor relief had reduced agricultural laborers to the position of "serfs and villeins on the soil."[7] The tone of this assault on the administrative techniques of paternalism was perhaps most effectively captured in one of Senior's several essays on the Old Poor Law:

> The great motive of the framers of the earlier English Poor Laws was to remedy the . . . class of inconveniences which affect, or appear to affect, the master. The motive of the framers of the later Acts, beginning with George the First, was to remedy the . . . class of evils which affect the free labourer and his family . . . [These laws] confined the labourer to his parish; they dictated to him who should be his master; and they proportioned his wages not to his services, but to his wants. Before the Poor Law Amendment Act, nothing but the power of arbitrary punishment was wanting in the pauperised parishes to a complete system of praedial slavery.[8]

---

[7] _Hansard_, 3rd series, XXIII (9 May 1834), 813-14, 821; XXIV (16 June 1834), 456. Also see _Fifth Annual Report of the Poor Law Commissioners_, P.P., 1839, XX, p. 12.

[8] _Historical and Philosophical Essays_, vol. II, p. 47. Quoted in Mackay, _A History of the English Poor Law_, III, pp. 11-13.

From this perspective, the only adequate poor law reform was one that would provide for the "independence" of labor. To be sure, such an object need not have disturbed even the most hidebound traditionalist. Men in the eighteenth century, too, idealized independent labor, which was most often expressed in the form of an appeal to the poor to secure subsistence without resort to charity or relief. Only rarely did this imply the desirability of competition or social fluidity in a period when status and deference were so deeply rooted in most men's conceptions of proper social organization.[9] Even in the early-nineteenth century, the notion of "independence" remained an equivocal ideal. In no sense did it sanction the right of the poor to conduct their affairs outside the pale of "morality" and the rule of property. Yet the nineteenth century attached a different meaning to "independence" than had the eighteenth, with its values of strict hierarchy and subordination of personal interests to the requirements of social harmony. This was a distinction that Richard Cobden had in mind when he contrasted the paternal charity of the squire with the ideal of his own class:

> Mine is the masculine species of charity which would lead me to inculcate in the minds of the labouring classes the love of independence, the privilege of self-respect, the disdain of being patronized or petted, the desire to accumulate and the ambition to rise.[10]

For those of this bent -- and they did not only include "new men" such as Chadwick, Senior, and Cobden -- the reorganization of relief administration provided the opportunity to enshrine a "masculine species of charity" in law and to establish it as general public policy. In large measure, the amendment of the poor laws offered

---

[9] Poynter, Society and Pauperism, p. xviii.

[10] Quoted in Perkin, The Origins of Modern English Society, 1780-1880, p. 225.

the prospect of raising expectations among the lowest elements of the laboring population, of increasing the self-sufficiency and geographical mobility of the poor.[11] Even though the royal commissioners and their supporters did not echo Cobden in advocating upward mobility as a social ideal,[12] the burden of their argument implied the necessity of greater social fluidity, for the "creative," productive society they promised was dependent, to a considerable degree, upon the individual becoming detached from the restraints of communal custom and the imperatives of close personal relationships.[13] For Senior, Chadwick, and those who thought like them, free contract in labor gave the individual ownership of himself, proprietorship of his person and capacities, the only means by which the poor might find escape from "praedial slavery."[14]

The "liberation" of labor was not, of course, a prescription for anarchy and equality, both of which for contemporaries came to pretty much the same thing. When labor is treated as a commodity like any other factor of production, society becomes subject to a special type of control and organizing principle. Market relations compel their human participants to seek their livelihood by selling something on the market, in the case of workers their labor.[15] Because the need to compete for employment is universal and continuous in such circumstances, the market constitutes an impersonal and invisible system of compulsion that does not threaten society by recourse to naked force.[16] The distribution of rewards to labor in accordance with the standards of market behavior enforces on the workers a discipline of sobriety, frugality, and, above all, industry, which for royal

---

11 Bowley, Nassau Senior and Classical Economics, pp. 303-05.

12 Lubenow, The Politics of Government Growth, p. 67.

13 See Robert A. Nisbet, Tradition and Revolt: Historical and Sociological Essays (New York, 1970), p. 138.

14 Poynter, Society and Pauperism, p. 304.

15 George Dalton, Economic Systems and Society (Harmondsworth, 1974), pp. 36-37.

16 C.B. Macpherson, The Political Theory of Possessive Individualism (Oxford, 1967), p. 59.

commissioners and government spokesmen alike was one guarantee of social equilibrium. "Bad as the moral results of . . . bad physical conditions are," Chadwick later explained, "they would be far worse, but for the effect of one great important sedative and corrective element, namely bodily labour, the bodily labour necessary to obtain subsistence."[17] A similar nostrum for the "moral" regeneration of labor, also characterized by a reliance on the "sedative" and "corrective" effects stemming from the need of individuals to secure subsistence on the open market, was central to the royal commission's call for a deterrent workhouse system.[18]

The argument for market discipline was not so crude as older notions concerning "the utility of poverty," that want was desirable simply as a spur to industry and obedience. A free market in labor carried with it the more substantial promise that the reintegration of society would proceed from the substitution of contractual relations between employer and employed for the conscious, manipulative techniques of rule associated with values of social reciprocity. Only by providing sufficient scope for the identity of interests inherent in an unfettered economy could society, it seemed, reinforce the process that bound men together as the buyers and sellers of labor.[19] This, far more than the studied regimen of paternal relations, would satisfy the requirements of cohesion in an era of apparent social disintegration. The prime consideration was to conform to, rather than resist, the changes that had resulted in the "proletarianization" of the agricultural workers. The commissioners' remedies not only recognized the existence of these changes, but were proposed with the expectation that appropriate adjustments in relief administration could turn the altered circumstances of rural labor to the

---

17 Edwin Chadwick, "Physical and Moral Condition of the English Wage-Classes," 6 June 1865, Box #86, Chadwick Papers. See Hansard, 3rd series, XXV (21 July 1834), 231.

18 See supra, pp. 145-46.

19 See Senior, Three Lectures on the Rate of Wages, p. vi. Supra, pp. 95-96.

benefit and security of the entire community.[20]

It is a measure of the significance of poor law reform in 1834 that these proposed remedies threatened, in a direct way, the basic framework of what I have called the deference model. When society is conceived to be organic, made up of unequal orders with diverse functions and responsibilities and organized for a mutual objective, economic activity takes its place among other forms of moral behavior.[21] Rather than the sum of individual economic decisions expressed in a multitude of prior and conditional agreements, the organization of labor consists of an "authoritative allocation" of work and rewards, the appropriateness of which is determined by communal expectations or the decisions of local ruling elites.[22] This provides a wide field for the personal judgement of patrons in which merit is assessed on the basis of the individual's contribution to the good of society or his needs as a component of the social organism.[23] The market model, in contrast, subordinates this kind of personal judgement to the operation of an automatic mechanism of exchange in which merit is determined by the action of persons in pursuit of their own self-interest.[24] Work and rewards are not made available with regard for the common purpose of society nor are they tailored to the social function of labor.[25] Interpersonal relationships are undoubtedly found, but ideally they are devoid of moral content, based on the abstract and impersonal relations of contract.[26] This is what Edward

---

20 P.L.C. Report of 1834, Pelican edn., pp. 144-52, 341-53.

21 R.H. Tawney, Religion and the Rise of Capitalism (New York, 1954), pp. 19-20.

22 Macpherson, The Political Theory of Possessive Individualism, pp. 48-49.

23 Ibid., p. 64; Perkin, The Origins of Modern English Society, 1780-1880, p. 224.

24 Tawney, Religion and the Rise of Capitalism, pp. 19-20.

25 Macpherson, The Political Theory of Possessive Individualism, p. 51.

26 See Robert A.Nisbet, The Quest for Community

Thompson means when he refers to the "demoralizing" aspect of market values.[27]

For this reason, the royal commissioners' commitment to competition, contractual relations, and self-interest in economic behavior was bound to result in violent objections to their proposals from those who continued to adhere to the deference model. When the Whigs came forward with their poor law amendment bill, critics both in and out of Parliament couched their opposition in terms of a defense of the traditional, moral social order.[28] Underpinning their argument was a plea for the natural order of custom, the social responsibilities of landed property, and the religious teachings and historical precedents that sanctioned the poor's right to adequate relief. Clearly, there was an element of futility in such attempts to cling to a world that was rapidly passing, but William Lubenow has gone so far as to compare this opposition to "the paranoid style" in American politics, maintaining that critics of the New Poor Law were irrational, extreme, and confused.[29] This perspective is inadequate for at least two reasons. First, it too easily assumes that the royal commission's prescriptions were more realistic, less extravagant, and in general superior means for dealing with problems of poverty than those of their opponents. In view of the work of Mark Blaug, no such assumption can be safely made, for he has revealed a whole range of virtues in the Old Poor Law.[30] But more importantly, Lubenow's characterization underestimates the extent to which "the principles of 1834" represented a genuine challenge to traditional precepts of social order. The market's control of any of a number of economic activities must ultimately impinge in some way upon the organization of

---

(New York, 1953), p. 52.

27 "The Moral Economy of the English Crowd in the Eighteenth Century," p. 89.

28 Lubenow, The Politics of Government Growth, pp. 44, 182-83.

29 Ibid., pp. 66, 183, 185.

30 See "The Myth of the Old Poor Law and the Making of the New," pp. 151-84.

society. This is most obvious in the case of labor, since its disposition concerns one of the essential features of social intercourse. To place labor within the pale of the market mechanism ensures that such intercourse will be subordinated to the laws of the market. Economy will no longer be "embedded" in social relations, but rather the reverse.[31] This must necessarily compromise the control of elites over the fundamental relations of society, which is why those who have relied on the deference model as a social ideal have invariably regarded the advance of market relations as a very real threat to their rule, the stability of society, and the shape of the moral universe.[32] The historical significance of their fears and resistance to change of this sort cannot be ignored or rendered invalid by taking a condescending view of their principles and objectives.

Among other things, the tone of the opposition to the New Poor Law reminds us once again that older social ideals continued to have practical life in the early-nineteenth century. At the bottom of society, memory and oral tradition kept alive the values of mutuality, regardless of changes in the material condition of the poor and their relations with those in authority. Indeed, as we have seen, a growing divergence between widely-held ideals and reality constituted a potent source of conflict in the countryside by the late-eighteenth century. To this extent, at least, popular culture had become distinct from the outlook of polite society, agrarian capitalism and the political interests of the great already having eroded much of the substance of paternalism as an organizing principle of society. Still, the high visibility of the judicial powers of the large landowners in their capacity as magistrates provided the entire community with a means of assessing the actions of the rulers against older standards of conduct. Within this context, prescriptions of "goodness" continued to exert a considerable residual influence on gentry

---

31 Polanyi, The Great Transformation, pp. 57, 71.

32 Newby, "The Deferential Dialectic," pp. 150-51, 164.

behavior, if only because the realities of parochial life and opinion discouraged overt denials of social accountability. So too, the values of an idealized past found expression when vehement objections to the methods and implications of poor law reform gathered force in and out of Parliament in 1834. This opposition represented something more than the lament of a backwoods squire not yet reconciled to the passing of a society over which his ancestors had presided for centuries, or the nostalgic glance backward of an antiquarian caught up in the toils of an uncongenial urban environment. Rather, it gave voice to the deepest convictions of many men of standing who were engaged in a vital debate on the way in which England was to be governed and the extent to which the rulers of society should be prepared to make concessions to the pressures of rapid and manifold change.

The fact remains, nonetheless, that the appeal of the opposition argument was strictly limited, the New Poor Law passing through Parliament with large majorities and receiving the backing of most of the gentry when it was introduced into the agrarian counties. Traditionally, students of poor law reform have largely attributed this overwhelming support to the burden of the rates on property. The New Poor Law has been depicted as a concession to the economic plight of farmers, a plan designed specifically to suit the financial interests of the "middling classes," and a means calculated to protect the rent rolls of the large landowners.[33] Even the decision of most Conservative M.P.s to support the Whig measure has been portrayed in such terms. Although these men were among those most wedded to customary institutions and practices, in the end, we are told, they "clearly voted against their prejudices and in favor of their

---

[33] U.R.Q. Henriques, "How Cruel Was the Victorian Poor Law?" Historical Journal, XI, 2 (1968), p. 370; E.C. Midwinter, Social Administration in Lancashire, 1830-1860 (Manchester, 1969), pp. 9, 58; M. Bruce, The Coming of the Welfare State (London, 1965), pp. 46-47; G.E. Mingay, intro., The Agricultural State of the Kingdom, p. xv; Hasbach, A History of the English Agricultural Labourer, p. 186.

purses."[34]

If nothing else, the findings of this study seem to stand squarely in the way of a simple line of explanation for the coming of the New Poor Law: rising rates and falling profits -- increasing complaints of farmers and landowners -- an act to reduce rates and to provide the conditions necessary for the stepped-up exploitation of labor. Admittedly, it is impossible to quarrel with the view that an increasing rate burden in the early-nineteenth century was instrumental in altering attitudes toward the poor.[35] In the years following the Napoleonic Wars, especially, the demands of public charity seemed a galling drain on the resources of the agricultural interest. The decline in wheat prices, coincidental with unprecedented relief expenditure in the period from 1817 to 1819, provoked fears that the rate burden was progressive and the kind of abolitionist sentiments that the Liverpool administration found so troubling. When relief costs began to fall in the early-1820s, prices fell even faster, so even then little satisfaction was found in the fact that the upward trend in expenditure had been halted. Nevertheless, by 1823 the Old Poor Law had weathered the most serious and convincing charges of financial abuses in its administration that it was ever to face. Despite a second rise in expenditure after the mid-1820s, the rate of increase was less steep than it had been previously, and the cost of relief never returned to its post-war oppressiveness.[36] Expenditure per head, too, remained well below post-war levels as a result of a population increase of more than two million in the years between 1821 and 1831.[37] In the early-1830s, a predomi-

---

34 Roberts, Victorian Origins of the British Welfare State, p. 43.

35 Marshall, The Old Poor Law, 1795-1834, pp. 23-25.

36 In the years from 1817 to 1819 annual expenditure averaged about £7.5 million; in the early-1830s costs averaged approximately £6.7 million per annum. Webb, English Poor Law History: The Last Hundred Years, Pt. II, Vol. II, pp. 1037-38.

37 Expenditure per head in 1818 (the worst year) stood at 13 shillings; in 1832, the year of the royal

nantly landowning Parliament continued to complain of the weight of taxation, but the belief that poor relief represented a progressively onerous obligation was not nearly as compelling or pervasive as it had been.[38] Government waste, the malt tax, and the state of the currency were more likely to be counted among the economic grievances of the agricultural interest than the cost of supporting the poor.[39]

The failure of the rates to rise in accordance with the principles of Malthusian analysis also affected the debate on the poor laws in 1834. In pointing to the rate burden as a justification for reform, the royal commission was forced to resort to special pleading: the post-war years saw extraordinary distress, necessitating uncharacteristically high expenditure; in the meantime the price of food had declined more sharply than relief, so in real terms the latter was more profuse than it had been before; the hidden subsidy to wages was far more prevalent in 1834 than in the second decade of the century.[40] Although such reasoning undoubtedly reflected and reinforced the convictions of those who regarded relief costs as excessive, the commissioners were careful not to press this line of argument too far. Instead, they preferred to stress the "moral mischief" of high rates in corrupting labor; here, they claimed, was the true source of "ultimate ruin."[41] Since the level of the rates had generally come to be regarded as a valid indicator of social malaise, such an approach was certain to be more effective in influencing public and parliamentary opinion than one that focused too obviously on trends in expenditure.[42]

---

commission's appointment, it was 9 shillings 7 pence, falling to 8 shillings 10 pence in 1833. Marshall, _The Old Poor Law, 1795-1834_, p. 26.

[38] Poynter, _Society and Pauperism_, p. 295.

[39] See, e.g., _Hansard_, 2nd series, XXII (4 March 1830), 1246-53; and XXIII (18 March 1830), 475-538.

[40] S.G. and E.O.A. Checkland, intro., _P.L.C. Report of 1834_, Pelican edn., p. 41.

[41] _P.L.C. Report of 1834_, Pelican edn., p. 476.

[42] Poynter, _Society and Pauperism_, p. 17.

This is not to deny that among the foremost attractions of poor law reform was its promise of substantial savings in relief at a time when the agrarian sector continued to suffer from the problems of surplus population. The nature of the commissioners' scheme for the transformation of labor, however, makes it difficult to see their recommendations as specially designed to satisfy the economic grievances of any particular group, including the landed interest. Since the commissioners envisaged a rise in wages and an end to the system of subsidization whereby ratepayers who did not employ labor were forced to share in its costs, their recommendations offered some economic advantage to everyone; the large farmers and proprietors were to reap their benefits from higher productivity, i.e., profits, not savings in the funds they were expected to make available to the laboring poor. While we can see that the array of proposals rooted in this rationale ultimately suited the needs of those who wished to secure the economic interests of property at the expense of the poor, it is equally clear that the Whigs were not numbered among them. The strength of ministerial resistance to Brougham's ambitions to restrict public aid reveals the extent to which relief expenditure per se was a secondary consideration for the government. It has been shown that from the start their attention was directed to questions concerning the conditions of labor and the state of order in the countryside. Only the elaboration of a scheme that took into account the economic plight of the poor could have induced the Whigs to promote a measure that also included plans to reduce the rates. Likewise, Parliament's reaction to the amendment bill was the expression of a virtual consensus of opinion on the poor laws which transcended the greed of grasping landlords or the selfishness of hard-pressed ratepayers in the arable-farming areas of the south. The reformers were able to draw on a full field of support, from outright opponents of the landed interest to those traditionalists who in most circumstances might have been expected to put their "prejudices" before their purses.[43]

---

[43] Lubenow, The Politics of Government Growth, pp. 41-42.

This does not mean that the debates on poor law reform were devoid of references to agricultural depression or the economic condition of the country. What is especially noteworthy about such references, however, is that they sprang chiefly from government arguments and were pressed for reasons of political expediency. When the Whigs took office in 1830, they pledged themselves to a policy of retrenchment in the face of serious financial difficulties that had helped to undermine the previous government. With the national debt absorbing more than a third of gross public expenditure, the task of devising economies was, in the words of Lord Holland, "no bed of roses."[44] Almost immediately the Whigs found demands for substantial reductions in government spending to be largely incompatible with fiscal responsibility and the necessities of day-to-day administration. "I am afraid it is too true," Grey told his son, Lord Howick, "that without a reduction of our debt and establishments, both nearly impossible to any great amount, nothing in the way of effectual [tax] relief can be looked for."[45] The true dimensions of the problem became even more apparent with the failure of Althorp's 1831 budget to gain the support necessary for a revamping of government finances.[46] From then on, the government was reduced to a "hand-to-mouth" financial policy, which included greater reliance on indirect taxation as a source of revenue.[47]

Increasingly, the pitfalls of this policy assumed critical proportions as the agricultural interest stepped up its agitation for tax relief, 1832 marking the return of bumper-crop years and low wheat prices after the poor harvests and more buoyant prices of the period from 1828

---

44 Lord Holland/Lord Grey, 16 November 1830, Box 34/2, Grey Papers; H. Roseveare, The Treasury: The Evolution of a British Institution (London, 1969), p. 187.

45 Lord Grey/Lord Howick, 16 January 1831, Box 25/2, Grey Papers.

46 Brock, The Great Reform Act, p. 134.

47 N. Gash, Reaction and Reconstruction in English Politics, 1832-1852 (Oxford, 1965), p. 177.

to 1831.[48] In 1833, the Whigs were defeated on a motion to repeal or reduce the malt tax, despite Althorp's plea that the government could not do without such an important source of revenue; only Sir Robert Peel's cooperation enabled them later to overturn the vote.[49] Even then, Althorp was forced into agreeing to the appointment of two select committees to investigate the state of the agrarian and industrial economies, although he continued to argue that "the expectations of the country on the subject of a redress of grievances in the way desired [lower taxes and currency reform] were impossible."[50] In the following year, on 21 February, the government again narrowly avoided defeat (202 Ayes to 206 Noes) on a motion to relieve the agricultural interest through a remission of taxes. By this time, however, the government had discovered in its poor law amendment bill a convenient adjunct to its haphazard financial policy, which Althorp was quick to offer as an answer to his critics on the matter of agrarian distress: he was aware, he said, that

> the small taxes payable off land were vexatious, but they did not take much from the farmer; and far greater benefit . . . would accrue from placing the poor-rates on an improved footing, than from anything that could be done in the way of relieving the landed interest from the pressure of direct [sic] taxes. Even the Malt-tax, of which so much had been said, would not afford the relief that was imagined. . . .[51]

In portraying poor law reform as a response to the economic ills of the country, the Whigs found themselves

---

48 Blaug, "The Myth of the Old Poor Law and the Making of the New," p. 162.

49 D. Spring, "Lord Chandos and the Farmers, 1818-1846," Huntington Library Quarterly, XXXIII, 3 (1970), p. 264.

50 Hansard, 3rd series, XVII (3 May 1833), 958.

51 Ibid., XXI, 663.

in an exposed and vulnerable position. Only a year earlier, they had reacted to demands for currency reform by denying the existence of severe or widespread distress; in order to make their case, they had pointed out that annual poor relief costs averaged "only" about £6,300,000 and that per-capita expenditure had declined some 26 percent between 1821 and 1831.[52] The abandonment of this position for one that touted poor law reform as a financial measure was not accomplished without some embarrassment for the government. The essentially opportunistic nature of this shift in outlook was effectively laid bare in the debate of 21 February by Edward Cayley with a pair of rhetorical questions:

> The noble Lord [Althorp] proposed to relieve the agriculturists by some alteration of the Poor-laws . . . But was it to relieve agricultural distress that an amendment in the Poor-laws was first proposed? Had not the Poor-law commissioners sat two or three years; whilst it was only last Session, or the beginning of this, that the House could be prevailed upon to acknowledge the existence of distress?[53]

Later, questions were also raised about the apparent contradiction between government claims that poor law reform meant both financial relief for property and economic benefits for the poor. When asked how the proposed measure would "do good to the landed interest if it did not diminish the amount of money to be given to the labourer," Althorp could only reply that it would "improve the condition of the farmer, by improving the habits of the labourer."[54] While this view accorded perfectly with the rationale of the royal commission's report, it was far more convoluted in its promise of

---

52 Ibid., XVII (22 April 1833), 1405.
53 Ibid., XXI, 674.
54 Ibid., XXIV (1 July 1834), 1059.

agrarian relief than Brougham's crude depiction of the amendment bill as a means to protect property from the claims of the poor, a characterization that remained unacceptable to his colleagues even when they expressed their opinions privately.[55]

It is significant that politicians most closely associated with the agricultural interest were among those who voiced serious doubts as to the economic benefits of reform. Lord Chandos, the Farmers' Friend who made a career of "deliberately and systematically" cultivating local rural opinion, remained entirely unconvinced that the Whigs' proposal offered an effective remedy for agricultural distress.[56] He even argued that the New Poor Law would actually increase financial burdens on the farmers and landowners as a result of the need to build workhouses.[57] Apparently, his rejection of Whig claims struck a responsive cord with those who were accustomed to following his lead in matters of this sort, for his periodic motions demanding tax relief for agriculture continued to draw substantial support even after the introduction of the government's poor law bill.[58] At a more exalted level of the Conservative party, Sir Robert Peel expressed similar doubts. Like Chandos, he considered the promise of savings in the rates to be "a delusion," for poor law abuses were "so manifold and so complicated" that "many years must elapse before any very perceptible improvement could be effected, or any great relief could be afforded to the agricultural interest."[59] Like the royal commission, he anticipated that under the New Poor Law funds currently used for poor relief would simply be converted to the payment of wages. When the poor law commission appointed under the amendment act came up for renewal in 1841, this is how he described his thinking

---

55 Ibid., XXIV (2 July 1834), 1072. See supra, p. 122.

56 Spring, "Lord Chandos and the Farmers, 1818-1846," pp. 259, 263.

57 Hansard, 3rd series, XXIV (7 July 1834), 1256.

58 Such a motion was defeated in the Commons by only 174 votes to 190 on 7 July 1834. Ibid., 1283.

59 Ibid., XXI (21 February 1834), 691.

in 1834:

> . . . what was the object of the amendment? That the virtuous and industrious labourer might receive and increase in the amount of his wages. He rejoiced, therefore, to hear that the amendment had had this very effect; that there had been no real saving, because of an addition to wages; and, indeed, that upon the whole the balance was against the employer and in favour of the employed. That was one great object for which he had hoped; he had supported the amendment with the desire that the labourer should receive an increase in the amount of his wages.[60]

In accepting the royal commission's vision of rising wages and greater industry, Peel adopted the view that property's real stake in reform was the improvement of "the moral condition of the poor" rather than the possibility of securing reductions in the amount of capital expended in support of labor; this was a position that he consistently held to throughout the period from 1834 to 1841 and beyond.[61]

The rates question, then, was much more complicated and multifaceted than unadorned references to "selfishness and class interest" would suggest.[62] Without question, agitation for an alleviation of financial demands on agriculture had reached large proportions by 1834. Yet Malthusian fears of progressive increases in the poor

---

60 Ibid., LVI (8 February 1841), 414.

61 See ibid., XXXI (8 February 1836), 161-62; and XXXVI (27 February 1837), 1088-89.

62 See Henriques, "How Cruel Was the Victorian Poor Law?" p. 371. In making this statement I wish to emphasize the words "unadorned references" -- it seems to me undeniable that in the broadest sense, the New Poor Law appealed to essentially selfish instincts.

rates were no longer as credible as they had been before the cost of public aid became a relatively fixed charge. At the same time, strenuous efforts were made to present the New Poor Law as an economic boon for all groups in society. Although it is difficult not to suspect disingenuousness on the part of many of those who argued in this vein, the range and strength of parliamentary support for the measure contend against any attribution of wholesale greed and cynicism; despite the fact that the rate burden was regional rather than national and probably had its greatest economic impact on those with little political influence, i.e., the smaller ratepayers and owner-occupiers who did not employ labor, the desire for an overhaul of the relief system was all but general and deeply felt.[63] To be sure, when Parliament came to discuss the poor laws, the possibility of providing some relief for agriculture formed part of the case for reform. An examination of the poor law debates, on the other hand, reveals a complex situation in which the government had ample reasons of a political nature to take a stand on such grounds, while major spokesmen for the agricultural interest were convinced that rate reductions were not likely to be among the chief benefits of reform. It is impossible, in short, to avoid the conclusion that the weight of the poor rates is not sufficient alone to account for the shape of the New Poor Law and the motivations of those in Parliament who embraced it.

In order to devise a more complete (and satisfactory) explanation for poor law reform, it is necessary to bear in mind that reform carried with it implications that went to the very heart of social relations in the countryside. As a result, the response of the political aristocracy to the royal commission's version of reform can tell us something about the way in which England's rulers perceived their society in 1834 and the course they wished to see it take in the future. Certainly we must be careful not to equate, as the Webbs did, huge majorities in Parliament with apathy or an uncritical acceptance of

---

63 Poynter, Society and Pauperism, p. 19.

Whig proposals.[64] The Conservative opposition's initial reaction to the amendment bill was by no means auspicious. Rumblings of dissatisfaction and alarm at the Carlton Club had reached the level of "a concurrence of opinion" before the Duke of Wellington and Sir Robert Peel were prevailed upon to put their influence behind the royal commission's recommendations.[65] Although these rumblings never came close to developing into a revolt against party leadership, they were serious enough to convince Peel that he would not have been able himself to introduce and carry such a measure if he had been in power.[66]

All the same, one is struck by the apparent ease with which this initial hostility to "the principles of 1834" was eventually allayed or brushed aside. This may in part be attributed to the substantial difficulties that critics faced in mounting an effective opposition. When the Grey administration presented the amendment bill to Parliament and the country, they were armed to the teeth with the royal commission's exhaustive report, the arguments of which both government spokesmen and opposition leaders echoed in debate with apparent conviction. As if this were not enough, the bill itself, the result of weeks of consultation between the cabinet and the royal commission, proved to be a particularly elusive target; the lack of specific provisions concerning relief policy, which was to be left to the new poor law commissioners to work out, especially hampered opponents in focusing their arguments.[67] But most important of all, critics were confronted with the need to fashion, in a limited time, elaborate responses to each of the royal commission's major propositions, for the credibility of those who opposed all or part of the government measure was largely dependent upon their being able to offer

---

64 Webb, English Poor Law History: The Last Hundred Years, Pt. II, Vol. I, p. 94.

65 William Sturges Bourne/Edwin Chadwick, 6 March 1834, Chadwick Papers.

66 Hansard, 3rd series, LVI (8 February 1841), 409.

67 Edsall, The Anti-Poor Law Movement, pp. 11-12, 14.

attractive alternatives: forthright defenses of the status quo were no longer acceptable.[68] The significance of this factor may be seen in the efforts of Sir Charles Burrell to secure approval for a labor rate scheme at the same time the poor law amendment bill was before Parliament. The vehement opposition of both the government and the royal commission to Burrell's measure ensured that those who positively supported the government's bill would refuse to back Burrell, even if they were sympathetic to the labor rate tradition. Sir Harry Verney, for example, declared himself "favourable to the general principle" of Burrell's proposal, but he declined to vote for it because it might "clash" with the poor law amendment bill, which he hoped would be brought to a "successful issue."[69] In the event, Burrell's measure was defeated on its second reading by a vote of 80 to 36. If this seems decisive, it should be recalled that the government's bill passed its second reading by 319 votes to 20. That is to say, when actually offered an alternative, however feeble, the Commons gave it almost twice the support they were willing to accord a simple negative vote on the government's poor law scheme, and that in a house only one-third as full.

In addition to suggesting that support for the amendment bill may not have been as solid as division lists would appear to indicate, the Burrell matter is a reminder of the extent to which options concerning reform of the relief system seemed to have narrowed. Although parliamentary tampering with the relief system in the early-1830s had never gone beyond experimentation with mere palliatives, this experience played a crucial role in preparing the ground for a comprehensive revision of relief administration. By 1834 the royal commission was able to draw on a large reservoir of frustration and hopelessness concerning poor law reform, which served to discourage opposition and to counteract misgivings. From the moment the New Poor Law was introduced to Parliament, the government took the position that the poor law

---

68 See Hansard, 3rd series, XXIII (14 May 1834), 962.

69 Ibid., XXIV (4 June 1834), 153.

question had boiled down to a simple choice between the proposed measure and "leaving things as they were."[70] Throughout the subsequent debates on the amendment bill, especially during its second reading in the Commons, many members registered grave reservations about some of the fundamental provisions of the bill but then proceeded to vote for it regardless.[71] W. Benett, for instance, announced his support for the measure in the same breath he condemned the workhouse system, "which only perpetuated poverty, [and which] must be abolished"; he justified his assent by arguing that what was most important was that "something must be done," that Parliament could no longer avoid some kind of decisive action.[72] While this was perhaps among the more extreme cases of desperation and muddled thinking, there was throughout Parliament a determination to legislate "at whatever hazard" (to use Althorp's words) before another session passed, a sentiment summed up by Joseph Hume, who himself had serious qualms about the powers to be given the poor law commissioners: when men are "sinking to the bottom of the abyss," he declared, it is necessary that they "catch at straws."[73]

It is here, in this prevailing sense of urgency and impending disaster, that we find a key source of the ground swell of support that greeted the New Poor Law in 1834 and after. For decades men had sought to understand the periodic crises that attended socio-economic change and, in seeking remedies, had given much attention to the poor laws as a central element in a social and economic system that gave rise to what seemed to be an ever-widening circle of distress. Although some observers had come, by the beginning of the nineteenth century, to see the relief system as an inexorable engine of misery and decay, those in charge of government preferred to treat each crisis as temporary and to devise temporary expedients to

---

70 Ibid., XXII (17 April 1834), 880.

71 Ibid., XXIII (9 May 1834), 805-42.

72 Ibid., 837.

73 Ibid., 831-37. See Lansdowne's comments, supra, p. 139 ; and Peel's in Hansard, 3rd series, XXVIII (25 May 1835), 111.

deal with it.[74] With the advent of unprecedented social upheaval in fielden England, and of heightened feelings of insecurity born of large-scale, direct assaults on the authority and property of provincial rulers, the discussion of the poor laws was transformed. Where once there had been sharp disagreement between those who wished to abolish the relief system and those who were determined to preserve its essential framework, now there was consensus on the need for comprehensive reform as Whig government and Conservative opposition joined hands in proclaiming current relief administration to be "a cancer eating into the vitals of the country."[75] The force of this argument was sustained by a conviction that authority now faced permanent danger, a conviction that found expression in fears for the future if a more effective discipline was not imposed on the laboring poor. Concessions to riot seemed to have compromised the rule of law, degraded the "character" of the workers, and placed a further burden on the limited resources of property. And with the widest publicity the royal commission trumpeted a terrible message in a society lacking credible instruments of coercion, that the administration of the poor laws mirrored and reinforced a residual paternalist ideal which could not be relied upon to ensure order and the safety of property. Even though such an ideal was predicated on deference and subordination, reaffirming its other imperatives could only become an additional source of discontent whenever and wherever authority failed to conform to its proper role. In taking steps to protect society from the dislocations of a market economy, it was as though the Speenhamland justices had so disrupted rural life as to have endangered society in other, more fearful ways.[76]

---

[74] Poynter, Society and Pauperism, pp. xxiii, 28-29.

[75] The words are Peel's, Hansard, 3rd series, LVI (8 February 1841), 408-09. This view was shared by the Duke of Wellington, ibid., XXXVII (7 April 1837), 851.

[76] Polanyi, The Great Transformation, pp. 3-4.

If some gentry continued to find economic advantage in the relief system as a means to maintain a cheap, subsidized labor force, by the 1830s the social disadvantages of their direct personal involvement in poor law administration had become too obvious to ignore. Even though the bulk of the laborers did not encounter the gentry as employers, the landlords' emerging control of relief administration made them seem more immediately responsible for the laborers' conditions of life. For this reason, in part, personal interaction between magistrate and laborer became one of the rural flash points in the troubled years of the early-nineteenth century. When the indignities of day-labor, of prolonged dependence on the ratepayers, of encroachments upon customary rights became too much for the laborers to bear, the gentry also shared in suffering popular reprisals, the targets of which were selected on the basis of perceived responsibility for the degradation of the poor. So far from reflecting the insulation of the landlords from the periodic crises that swept rural England after 1795, such breakdowns in social cohesion were fueled by greater individual activism on the part of some of the gentry and their meager attempts to maintain an image as protectors of the humble. Under the terms of the deference model, gestures of paternalism have to be authentic and substantive, unless authority is prepared to rule like a conquering army. The ultimate "crisis of paternalism," and, by the same token, of the Old Poor Law, rested in the fact that the intrinsic meaning of paternalism no longer retained that clear relevance to empirical reality that is a prerequisite of all effective ideals.[77]

Although the Whig ministers seem to have grasped this by the end of 1830, if not before, they could not be certain about how deep disillusionment with old administrative techniques had gone with other lawmakers and provincial rulers. As a result, Althorp showed notable restraint in his statements when asking leave to introduce

---

[77] The term is Edward Thompson's, "Patrician Society, Plebian Culture," passim. See Nisbet, Tradition and Revolt, p. 53.

the poor law amendment bill. Even though he did acknowledge, almost apologetically, that the complexity of the poor law problem required the establishment of "a new and a great power in the country,"[78] he was careful to stress that the proposed legislation was founded on the experience of workhouse administration in many parishes and the practical knowledge gleaned from such "experiments."[79] Even the generally favorable reaction to this claim was not enough to calm government fears that a powerful opposition might spring up at any moment, Althorp telling Senior that he was not at all confident about "the safety of the measure" when it should come to be debated in the Commons.[80] Accordingly, soon after, the cabinet decided to withdraw from the draft bill itself "those expressions . . . which most pointedly directed attention towards the Workhouse, or enabled the Commissioners to enforce the Workhouse system. . . ."[81] Similar caution later induced the government to make several "popular concessions" to criticism, such as limiting the term of the poor law commission to five years, despite the continued failure of opponents to attract significant backing.[82]

Obviously, the strength of these apprehensions provided an ample motive to minimize the novelty of reform, to portray the New Poor Law as the mere culmination of administrative practices and principles which had evolved over the preceding decades. Consequently, in characterizing contemporary perceptions of what reform implied, the government's public statements in this regard should be viewed with some skepticism.[83] Even

---

78 This was a reference to the poor law commission.

79 Hansard, 3rd series, XXII (17 April 1834), 879-80.

80 N.W. Senior, "Poor Law Amendment Bill Conferences," n.d., London University Library MS. 173, p. 72.

81 Ibid., p. 73. The preamble to the 45th clause of the bill was removed; this stated that all able-bodied paupers should be relieved in a workhouse.

82 Ibid., p. 78. See also pp. 99-100.

83 See, e.g., Lubenow, The Politics of Government Growth, p. 56.

so impolitic an individual as Edwin Chadwick recognized the need to soft-pedal the innovative features of the amendment bill, especially the provisions for a central authority in relief affairs. "This is an Assumption of Power," he warned, "which will probably excite Opposition, unless it is very carefully guarded in introducing it to the Public."[84] In private, on the other hand, proponents of reform could be unabashedly open with one another about the novelty of their scheme. "Such an accumulation of powers, legislative, judicial, & administrative," Senior said of the proposed poor law commissioners, "was never before intrusted [sic] to any functionaries. And for their guidance in all these duties they have no precedent."[85] More importantly, even in their public statements Whig ministers did not consistently shrink from provocative arguments. Once the cabinet realized that Parliament was prepared for strong medicine, the government grew bolder in its assertions; certainly by the time the bill reached the Lords, after having progressed triumphantly through the Commons, the government position was much tougher and more decisive than it had been only a few months earlier when Althorp had been anxious to avoid references to innovation and dislocation. In part this was because Brougham was in charge of the bill in the Lords, and he, of course, showed none of Althorp's prudence:

> My Lords, I am perfectly aware that such powers as these [which are to be committed to the poor law commissioners] may be designated as unconstitutional. I am aware that at any rate they are . . . novel, as vested in one Board . . . My Lords, if this be a great step, -- if this be an extraordinary enactment, -- if this be an unheard-of measure which

---

84 Original draft, Notes of Heads of a Bill, 1833, p. 17, Box #18, Chadwick Papers.

85 N. Senior/Lord Melbourne, 30 June 1834 (copy), Box #20, Chadwick Papers.

> we are now discussing, -- supposing I admit it all -- I ask, are not the times in which we live, in this respect, of an extraordinary aspect?[86]

But Brougham, while using strong language indeed, could not be accused, in this case at least, of deviation from the views of his colleagues. In pointing to desperate conditions as justification for Whig proposals, he was simply repeating a government line which had been used to good effect in the Commons. He was, in addition, not the only one prepared to characterize the provisions of the New Poor Law in such terms. Calling the establishment of the poor law commission "a most important part of the Bill," Earl Grey, the former Prime Minister, insisted that the gravity of the poor law problem required the government to confer on the commissioners "powers of a very extensive and extraordinary kind."[87]

It was with good reason that talk of "extraordinary" measures centered primarily on the administrative structure of the New Poor Law, as the provisions of the act were chiefly concerned with the reorganization of administrative mechanisms in some novel and striking ways. This is perhaps most obvious in the case of the central board of poor law commissioners, who were charged with fashioning and enforcing, for the first time, a national poor law policy. If their power did not prove to be as extensive and effective as Brougham and Grey claimed, the appointment of the commission necessarily required (and implied) the loss of some local authority and independence. This was especially so in light of the commissioners' intentions, supported by the royal commission's report and unequivocal government statements in the poor law debates of 1834, to root out the administrative diversity of the old system, which was seen as part of its "corrupt" character.[88] As the commissioners remarked

---

86 Hansard, 3rd series, XXV (21 July 1834), 241-43.

87 Ibid., XXV (11 July 1834), 14.

88 See ibid., XXIII (14 May 1834), 995.

in their sixth annual report, the Old Poor Law had been characterized by a systematic disregard for the formal provisions of the law, parish officers and magistrates being concerned with molding relief administration to conform to the circumstances of the moment and the needs of the local community. In contradistinction to this, the commissioners steeled themselves, as part of their principal mission and according to their parliamentary mandate, to confine "an abusive and lax administration within the strict limits of the law."[89] Although they were never able, for a variety of reasons, to implement such a policy, this avowed commitment to the rule of law carried with it a rejection of qualitative social and cultural differences and a desire to subordinate them to the claims of exact, consistent, and uniform regulations. It is precisely values of this sort that condition and mark the increasing bureaucratization of government and the administrative methods that sustain it.[90]

As significant as all this is for the history of central government, it must be emphasized that bureaucratic values did not solely inform the appointment and subsequent work of the poor law commissioners and those who were immediately responsible to them, the assistant commissioners, district auditors, and staff at Somerset House (a bureaucracy, in fact). Rather, the New Poor Law reorganized local administration in such a way as to infuse it with true bureaucratic elements in both its structure and operation. Direct day-to-day contact with the poor was delegated to a cadre of salaried functionaries with carefully prescribed duties, their continued employment being contingent upon their ability and

---

[89] Quoted in Lubenow, The Politics of Government Growth, pp. 59-60. See P.L.C. Report of 1834, Pelican edn., p. 82.

[90] Nisbet, Tradition and Revolt, p. 64. In identifying threats to cultural diversity, Max Weber regarded the development of bureaucracy as in some measure analogous to the "mechanical uniformity" that characterized the philosophical rationalism of the Enlightenment.

willingness to perform within established guidelines. In this vein, relieving officers, who were full-time professionals, replaced the part-time, amateur overseers of the poor, who for centuries had been chosen from the immediate community to fulfill what was essentially a communal, rather than an administrative, responsibility. At the policy-making and managerial level of local administration, vestries and the magistracy were likewise replaced by boards of guardians made up of elected ratepayers and magistrates sitting ex officio. In drawing upon the same sort of unpaid personnel who served in vestries and on the bench, boards of guardians may appear to have represented nothing more than a simple and convenient reconstitution of parochial government. But creation of the boards transformed a collection of haphazard, ad hoc jurisdictions and functions into a network of relatively uniform bodies with a permanent, on-going existence, regularized procedures, and some measure of accountability to central government. Among the consequences of such a transformation was the way in which it altered the judicial aspects of poor law administration. The purpose and effect of the New Poor Law, as Senior pointed out, was to convert the magistrates from judges into administrators.[91] This may seem a small change.[92] It is, in fact, a watershed in the history of authority.

As we have seen, the judicial role of the large landowners in poor law administration was the chief institutional expression of their personal responsibility for the subsistence of the community. While this responsibility was not always welcomed or acted upon, it did provide a source of popular patronage, which, like all patronage, involved a process of "selection by merit."[93] This, ideally, left ample room for those in

---

[91] N.W. Senior, Remarks on the Opposition to the Poor Law Amendment Bill (London, 1841), pp. 37-38, 42.

[92] William Lubenow argues that this conversion simply established the new administration in "the context of conventional social and political forms." The Politics of Government Growth, p. 59.

[93] The term is Harold Perkin's in The Origins of Modern English Society, 1780-1880, p. 224.

authority to make examples of the "undeserving" and to show mercy to the "deserving," for judgeship not only allowed discrimination; it insisted upon it as an essential element of landed rule.[94] As administrators, on the other hand, magistrates joined elected ratepayers to direct relief in parishes that had been brought together to form consolidated poor law unions. Although magistrates were always assured of a voice in board decisions by virtue of their ex officio status, the collective responsibility of board management for areas extending well beyond the influence of individual landowners undermined opportunities for the manipulation of popular patronage in the system.[95] At the same time, the corporate character of board management, involving as it did representation of different degrees and types of property, largely eliminated the judge's vital role in relief administration, since the new system, unlike the judicial process, did not require landlord participation, or even their presence in the neighborhood.[96]

Efforts to introduce more standardized, objective forms of administration were also reflected in the commitment of both the royal commissioners and the poor law commissioners to the universal application of a "workhouse test" of destitution. With deterrent workhouses to ensure that only the truly destitute would accept relief, administrators, the royal commission explained, need not trouble themselves with distinguishing between the "deserving" and "undeserving" poor, questions which were more properly left to private charity:[97]

> The offer of relief on the principle suggested . . . would be a self-acting test

---

94 Supra, p.67.

95 See P.L.C. Report of 1834, Pelican edn., pp. 417-18, 423, 439, 445-50; Alfred Power /Poor Law Commissioners, 20 July 1835, First Annual Report, 1835, App. B, No. 5, p. 137; Third Annual Report, 1837, p. 26; Henry Ashworth/ Edwin Chadwick, 8 Oct. 1836, Chadwick Papers.

96 See P.L.C. Report of 1834, Pelican edn., p. 419.

97 Blaug, "The Myth of the Old Poor Law and the Making of the New," pp. 152-53.

> of the claim of the applicant . . . By the means which we propose, the line between those who do and those who do not need relief is drawn, and drawn perfectly. If the claimant does not comply with the terms on which relief is given to the destitute, he gets nothing; and if he does comply, the compliance proves the truth of the claim -- namely, his destitution . . . no agency for contending against fraudulent rapacity and perjury, no stages of appeals (vexatious to the appellants [sic] and painful to the magistrates), be requisite to keep the able-bodied from the parish.[98]

In its ideal form, this was a procedure that precluded the niceties of discrimination and the vagaries of "selection by merit" which under the old system had provided judges with the means to elicit thankfulness or awe from those who had been compelled to place themselves at the discretion of authority. This in turn left no scope for the poor to appeal to the consciences and social responsibilities of administrators, for in addition to being "self-acting" and therefore impartial, the test placed the burden of decision on the poor themselves; as Geoffrey Finlayson has remarked, "simply by making his claim, the claimant examined himself."[99] The effect of all this could only be to "demoralize" relations between the administrators and recipients of relief, to remove public aid from the realm of mutuality, custom, and sentiment. In this sense, too, proposed poor law policies once again reinforced the objective of strengthening "amoral" market relations in the society at large, as the smooth operation of a market economy is impeded if ethical, emotional, and personal elements are allowed substantial rein in the conduct of official business.[100]

---

98 P.L.C. Report of 1834, Pelican edn., p. 378.

99 Decade of Reform: England in the Eighteen Thirties (New York, 1970), p. 56.

100 Nisbet, Tradition and Revolt, p. 65.

Without question, the need to convert judges into administrators sprang from a wide range of considerations, but among those most relevant to this discussion were contemporary perceptions of social conditions in the countryside. Vulnerable, isolated magistrates, it was thought, could not be relied upon to introduce stringent relief policies when they were certain to be resisted by force:

> Whatever may have been the various causes of the agricultural riots in various districts, [the royal commission claimed] . . . the one effect has been to prove that the discretion exercised in the distribution of the poor's rate can be effected [sic] by intimidation . . . if a gentleman living upon his own property were strictly to perform his duty in a large proportion of the cases where paupers appealed from their overseers, he would be in danger of having his property destroyed . . . to expect the voluntary execution of new and strict regulations by persons placed under such circumstances appears unreasonable.[101]

One solution to this problem was to strengthen the resources of order and to mobilize them for the purpose of introducing wholesome measures. The corporate authority vested in the boards of guardians and the spectacle and consolidation of power in each poor law union promised to bolster administrators and provide them with a degree of safety and instruments of coercion that had not been available to judges. "The very sight of a well-built efficient [workhouse]," an assistant poor law commissioner explained, "would give confidence to the Board of Guardians; the sight and weekly assemblage of all servants of their Union would make them proud of their office; the appointment of a chaplain would give dignity to the whole

---

101 P.L.C. Report of 1834, Pelican edn., pp. 408-09.

arrangement, while the pauper would feel it was utterly impossible to contend against it."[102] Of equal importance here was the need to shield community leaders from individual, personal responsibility for the introduction of a poor law system that by its very nature would violate a residual moral order, which, as judges, they were expected to uphold. While the less visible and exposed role of administrator provided magistrates with considerable benefits in this regard, the creation of a faceless, distant, and external authority seemed necessary to underline and maintain the impersonal character of the new system. A central board, the royal commission argued, would relieve administrators (since they, unlike judges, would come under governmental direction) from the sanctions of "local interests" and "affections": "The Commissioners would assist those who were willing to exert themselves in bringing about the change [in administration], and would exonerate from responsibility those . . . who could not sustain it beneficially. Since the Commissioners would have no local interests or affections, they would enforce the law without ill-temper on their parts, and without exciting animosity."[103]

Such an argument reveals a keen sense of the capacity of bureaucratic organization and procedures to provide an effective substitute for the discipline of traditional authority. Emphasis must be placed on the word "substitute," for the royal commission's view of proper poor law administration was largely incompatible with the imperatives of the deference model. The commissioners' administrative ideal, as they repeatedly made clear in their report, was corporate rather than personal, professional rather than amateur, regular rather than *ad hoc*, uniform rather than diverse, detached rather than communal, self-acting rather than discretionary, universal rather than specific. If only because of its variance from the deference model, it was an ideal that

---

[102] Ms. Minutes, Poor Law Commissioners, 3 Nov. 1834. See also Lubenow, *The Politics of Government Growth*, p. 61.

[103] *P.L.C. Report of 1834*, Pelican edn., p. 419. My emphasis.

suggested the need for a fundamental alteration in a vital part of the institutional framework that helped to hold society together. Even though contemporaries were not always fully aware of this (certainly Senior and Chadwick, at the very least, are exceptions here), and despite the fact that actual administration under the New Poor Law necessarily remained imperfect, the attempt to "rationalize" even limited aspects of authority was a major step in coping with the "transition process" that Harriet Martineau referred to in her 1844 letter to Lord Howick.[104] According to Robert Nisbet, the advance of bureaucracy, "however incomplete it must always be in actual operation," represents the emergence of a distinctive and historically identifiable form of control and restraint.[105] As authority becomes objectified and externalized, the abstract hierarchy of bureaucracy rather than personality and social status -- office rather than the individual -- increasingly mediate and define relations between rulers and the ruled. Those who hold office may exercise considerable power over the lives of other men, but it is not necessary that the administrator be trusted or believed in or that he be recognized, personally, as a leader of the immediate, circumscribed community.[106] The impact of this sort of development on the shape and organization of society is what Nisbet has in mind when he writes of "the state as revolution."[107]

In view of the implications of the proposals embodied in the New Poor Law, it is perhaps understandable that they were the end product of an unprecedented approach to the formulation of national poor law policy. Over the centuries the Old Poor Law had grown out of an ever-increasing collection of expedients, its legal structure reflecting local practices of long-standing or shifts in local opinion, which Parliament had moved, belatedly, to legitimize in the law.[108] Undoubtedly, the New Poor Law, too, combined

---

104 Supra, p. 11.
105 The Social Bond (New York, 1970), p. 124.
106 See Nisbet, Tradition and Revolt, p. 63.
107 The Quest for Community, p. 98.
108 Marshall, The Old Poor Law, 1795-1834, pp. 10-11.

several elements that had already been worked out in scattered parts of the country, including the incorporation of parishes, the use of deterrent workhouses, and the appointment of paid assistant overseers; and these examples performed the useful role of precedents to which the royal commission and the government were able to appeal. But by selecting, modifying, and synthesizing existing examples, the royal commissioners offered an authentically original solution to the poor law problem, original in the crucial sense that administrative structure and relief procedures were carefully coordinated to form a single, universal system in support of a comprehensive vision of ideal socio-economic relationships. It was a solution, moreover, that took its shape from the efforts and views of a relatively small group of individuals at the center of power and events. This is not to say that local authority did not have sufficient reasons to be enthusiastic about the New Poor Law, among which were desires to reduce the rates, to counter the "moral" effects of poor relief abuses, to avoid conflicts between magistrates and ratepayers, to strengthen the arsenal of coercive mechanisms available for use against the "unruly," to protect proprietors from communal expectations, to lighten or eliminate altogether the burden of administering public aid, to further the interests of agrarian capitalists, and, in some cases, to improve the lot of the poor. Nonetheless, being caught up in an increasingly difficult situation and often reacting to it in traditional ways, influential figures and officials in the localities (and most of their representatives in Parliament for that matter) generally lacked the perspective and resources necessary to fashion a systematic and all-embracing response to the poor law problem. This of course did not prevent them from voicing bitter complaints about relief administration or from producing a spate of reform suggestions, some of them well thought out, others hair-brained.[109] By the 1830s, however, these

---

[109] For an extensive discussion of ideas on poor relief in the pre-reform period, see Poynter, Society and Pauperism, passim.

complaints and suggestions had long been characteristic of a general dissatisfaction with relief administration, and their success in promoting change in national poor law policy had been notably limited. What was absolutely essential in this regard was the conversion of major political figures to the idea of reform, and this conversion, when it came, appears to have been one aspect of a mounting sense of crisis at the highest levels of government. Faced with this emergency, those in power then increasingly resorted to the advice of "experts," whose views on relief administration did not arise from close observation of local practice (despite their claims to the contrary) and whose commitment to reform did not spring from the pressures of local opinion.

The crisis that engulfed the Old Poor Law provided both the need and the opportunity to devise means to manipulate and moderate the forces of social change. It was not enough simply to narrow the range of government responsibility. What was required on the one hand was a positive act of destruction, one that in subjecting labor to the laws of the market would undermine noncontractual associations and preclude their spontaneous revival.[110] Given the climate and conditions of the time, to advocate the establishment of a national system of deterrent workhouses was to advocate an active policy of interference in organic forms of social organization. At the same time, the continued importance of the poor laws in mediating relations between property and the destitute required an act of creation in the readjustment of institutional forms of authority: professional central administration was offered as an alternative to the old combination of private legislation and local discretion; the greater consolidation and rationalization of local administration transformed older assumptions concerning government and social accountability; the report of 1834 provided the New Poor Law as a whole with a more rigorous and systematic theoretical foundation than that which had sustained the old system.[111]

---

110 Polanyi, The Great Transformation, p. 163.
111 Poynter, Society and Pauperism, p. xxii.

As J.D. Chambers and G.E. Mingay have noted, these and other similar acts of destruction and creation in this period were carried out "peacefully."[112] Indeed, the process described here was part of a general evolutionary trend spanning the century, which saw the supersession of informal and personal methods of government by those that were more institutional and bureaucratic, however incomplete and flawed in actual operation. It is also true, however, that this process was "peaceful" in only a limited sense, since by its very nature it wreaked havoc on a whole way of life at the bottom of society. Even as late as 1830, the response of local authority to social conflict left some room for the hope that problems would be resolved in ways that accorded with the minimal expectations of the poor. With government repression in the aftermath of Swing, and, above all, with the introduction of the New Poor Law in the counties, disillusionment became final and irreversible. Mutuality, even as myth, was revealed as meaningless once and for all. Until the laborers began to seek their own salvation in the trade union movement of the late-nineteenth century, they were left with no compelling principle with which to protect their interests or to order their relations with those who controlled the necessities of life. The "crisis of paternalism" had passed through its last agonies; all that was left was obedience or incendiarism and anonymous violence.

---

[112] The Agricultural Revolution, 1750-1880, p. 208.

Appendix A

List of the counties in order of relief expenditure per head of population for the year ending 25 March 1822.

*Indicates county or riding north of the Caird wage-line.

1. Sussex
2. Northamptonshire
3. Buckinghamshire
4. Essex
5. Kent
6. Oxfordshire
7. Suffolk
8. Bedfordshire
9. Huntingdonshire
10. Berkshire
11. Norfolk
12. Cambridgeshire
*13. Leicestershire
14. Wiltshire
15. Hertfordshire
16. Hampshire
17. Dorsetshire
18. Herefordshire
*19. Lincolnshire
20. Surrey
*21. Rutland
22. Middlesex
23. Warwickshire
*24. Westmorland
*25. East Riding (Yorks.)
26. Devonshire
*27. Durham
28. Gloucestershire
29. Shropshire
30. Worcestershire
*31. North Riding (Yorks.)
*32. Cheshire
33. Cornwall
*34. Derbyshire
*35. Northumberland
*36. Nottinghamshire
37. Somersetshire
*38. Staffordshire
*39. Cumberland
*40. West Riding (Yorks.)
*41. Lancashire

Source: Report from the Select Committee on Poor Rate Returns, P.P., 1823, V, App. D.2., p. 14.

	(1)	(2)	(3)	(4)	(5)	(6)	(7)	(8)
						Percentage of Parishes Answering Q. #43		
Counties	Total No. of Rural Parishes	Percentage of Rural Parishes Reporting	Total County Population in 1831 (in 000's)	Percentage of population reporting	Per-capita Relief Expenditure in 1831 (s.d.)	Magistrates Controlling Relief	Magistrates Not Controlling Relief	Magistrates Sometimes Controlling Relief
Sussex	313	27	275	69	19.4	77	15	8
Bucks.	230	16	148	23	18.7	81	15	4
Suffolk	525	10	299	20	18.4	63	37	-
Essex	413	12	321	31	17.2	85	15	-
Oxford	298	10	154	42	16.11	78	18	4
Beds.	141	12	96	12	16.11	64	18	18
Northants.	343	5	181	9	16.10	77	15	8
Wilts.	374	8	243	20	16.9	82	13	5
Berks.	222	16	147	27	15.9	74	22	4
Norfolk	753	6	394	10	15.4	65	31	4
Hunts.	107	13	54	18	15.3	80	10	10
Kent	421	13	484	25	14.5	62	26	12
Hants.	342	16	318	31	13.10	75	19	6
Cambridge	169	25	145	34	13.8	52	30	18
Herts.	147	13	145	23	13.2	43	50	7
Yorks. (E.R.)	365	3	205	5	11.11	33	67	-
Leicester	339	5	199	12	11.7	69	8	23
Dorset	305	5	161	7	11.5	82	9	9
Hereford	274	7	112	13	11.4	33	47	20
Lincoln	727	3	321	6	11.0	50	38	12
Surrey	146	18	491	12	10.11	75	25	-
Middlesex	80	1	1,373	0.6	10.1	50	50	-
Westmorland	116	17	56	5	9.8	34	53	13
Warwick	255	15	340	26	9.7	63	37	-
Devon	475	5	500	6	9.0	50	28	22
Somerset	493	5	409	16	8.10	71	29	-

continued/. . . .

Appendix B continued

Yorks. (N.R.	537	2	193	5	8.9	57	29	14
Gloucester	425	7	391	18	8.8	61	33	6
Shropshire	275	7	225	23	8.2	15	8	-
Worcester	241	8	214	49	7.6	41	53	6
Durham	297	13	257	49	6.10	52	43	5
Cornwall	212	15	304	19	6.8	44	44	12
Derby	331	2	240	0	6.8	25	25	50
Notts.	269	10	228	27	6.6	60	40	-
Stafford	345	4	415	13	6.6	38	50	12
Chester	500	3	338	2	6.3	14	72	14
Northumb.	524	4	181	13	6.3	30	60	10
York (W.R.)	666	9	987	36	5.7	69	21	10
Cumberland	294	16	127	26	5.6	46	50	17
Monmouth	157	6	99	13	5.5	33	50	17
Lancaster	444	4	1,352	4	4.5	9	73	18

Note: Rutland is not included because none of its reporting parishes (4) replied to question #43.

Sources

Columns 1 - 5: Mark Blaug, "The Poor Law Report Reexamined," Journal of Economic History, XXIV, 2 (June 1964), pp. 236-237.

Columns 6 - 8: Report from His Majesty's Commissioners for inquiring into the Administration and Practical Operation of the Poor Laws, Appendix B, Answers to Rural Queries, P.P., 1834, **XXXIII.**

BIBLIOGRAPHY

I. Personal Papers

University College, London

Bentham Papers
Brougham Papers
Chadwick Papers

British Library, London

Peel Papers
Holland House Papers
Ripon Papers

University of London Library

Nassau Senior MS.

Royal Archives, Windsor

Melbourne Papers

Bodleian Library, Oxford

Graham Papers (microfilm)

University of Durham, Durham

Grey Papers

John Rylands Library, Manchester

Kay-Shuttleworth Papers

Public Record Office, London

Russell Papers

II. Parliamentary Papers

Report from the Committee on Certain Returns Relative to the State of the Poor, 23 May 1787, P.P., 1816 (reprinted), IV.

Report on the Poor Laws of This Kingdom, P.P., 1816, IV.

Minutes of Evidence Taken Before the Lords Committee Appointed to Consider of the Poor Laws, P.P. (Lords), 1817 (43. of 1817), LXXIV.

Report from the Select Committee on the Poor Laws, P.P., 1817, VI.

Report of the Lords Committee on the Poor Laws, P.P. (Lords), 1817 (101. of 1817), LXXXIV.

First and Second Reports from the [Commons] Select Committee on the Poor Laws, P.P. (Lords), 1818 (62. of 1818), XCI.

Report from the Select Committee on the Education of the Lower Orders, P.P., 1818, IV.

Third Report from the Select Committee on the Poor Laws, P.P., 1819 (358.) [i.e., 1818], V.

Report from the Committee on the Poor Laws, P.P., 1819, II.

Report from the Select Committee . . . [on] the Depressed State of the Agriculture of the United Kingdom, P.P., 1821, IX.

Report from the Select Committee on Poor Rate Returns, P.P., 1821, IV.

Report from the Select Committee . . . [on] the Distressed State of the Agriculture of the United Kingdom, P.P., 1822, V.

List of All Petitions Presented to the House of Commons . . . Complaining of Agricultural Distress, P.P., 1822, V.

Second Report from the Select Committee . . . [on] the Depressed State of the Agriculture of the United Kingdom, P.P., 1822, V.

Report from the Select Committee on Poor Rate Returns, P.P., 1822, V.

Report from the Select Committee on Poor Rate Returns, P.P., 1823, V.

Report from the Select Committee on Labourers' Wages, P.P., 1824, VI.

Report from the Select Committee on Poor Rate Returns, P.P., 1824, VI.

Abstract of Returns Made to the Committee in 1824 Relative to Labourers' Wages, P.P., 1825, XIX.

Report from the Select Committee on Poor Rate Returns, P.P., 1825, IV.

Report from the Select Committee on Poor Rate Returns, P.P., 1826, III.

Report from the Select Committee on the Law of Parochial Settlements, P.P., 1828, IV.

Report from the Select Committee on That Part of the Poor Laws Relating to the Employment or Relief of Able-Bodied Persons from the Poor Rate, P.P., 1828, IV.

Report from the Select Committee . . . [on] Select and Other Vestries, P.P., 1830, IV.

Minutes of Evidence Taken Before the Select Committee of the House of Lords Appointed to Consider of the Poor Laws, P.P. (Lords), 1830-1 (19. of 1830-1), CCLXXXVII.

First Report of the Select Committee on the Poor Laws, P.P. (Lords), 1830-1 (30. of 1830-1), CCLXXXVII.

Third Report from the Select Committee on the Poor Laws, P.P. (Lords), 1830-1 (84. of 1830-1), CCLXXXVII.

Tabular Statement Showing the Comparative Ability of the Several Counties in England to Support Their Agricultural Population, P.P. (Lords), 1830-1 (58. of 1830-1), CCLXXXVIII.

Report from the Select Committee on the Silk Trade, P.P., 1831-2, XIX.

Return of the Number of Parishes in Each County in England and Wales, in which a Plan Has Been Agreed Upon by the Vestry and Approved by the Magistrates in Petty Sessions, for the Employment of the Poor of such Parish, under the Provisions of the Act 2 & 3 Will. IV, c. 96 [Labor Rate], P.P., 1833, XXXII.

Copy of the Letter Addressed by the Chancellor of the Exchequer to the Poor Law Commissioners . . . and of the Answer Returned by the Commissioners, P.P. (Lords), 1833 (71. of 1833), CCCXXIV.

Report from the Select Committee on Agriculture, P.P., 1833, V.

Copy of Any Documents in the Possession of the Poor Law Commissioners, With Regard to the Labour Rate Bill, P.P., 1833, XXXII.

Report from His Majesty's Commissioners for Inquiring into the Administration and Practical Operation of the Poor Laws. App. B, Answers to Rural Queries, P.P., 1834, XXXIII.

Report from the Select Committee on the State of Education, P.P., 1834, IX.

Report from the Select Committee on Education in England

and Wales, P.P., 1835, VII.

First Annual Report of the Poor Law Commissioners for England and Wales, P.P., 1835, XXXV.

First Report from the Select Committee . . . [on] the State of Agriculture, P.P., 1836, VIII.

Second Report from the Select Committee . . . [on] the State of Agriculture, P.P., 1836, VIII.

Third Report from the Select Committee . . . [on] the State of Agriculture, P.P., 1836, VIII.

Second Annual Report of the Poor Law Commissioners for England and Wales, P.P., 1836, XXIX.

Report from the Lords' Select Committee on the State of Agriculture in England and Wales, P.P., 1837, V.

Third Annual Report of the Poor Law Commissioners for England and Wales, P.P., 1837, XXXI.

Fourth Annual Report of the Poor Law Commissioners for England and Wales, P.P., 1837-8, XXVIII.

Return Showing the Size in Square Miles of the Several Unions, the Population, and Number of Guardians, P.P., 1837-8, XXXVIII.

Report from the Select Committee on Education of the Poorer Classes in England and Wales, P.P., 1838, VII.

Report from the Select Committee of the House of Lords Appointed to Examine into . . . the Operation of the Poor Law Amendment Act, P.P. (Lords), 1838, XXII, XXIII.

Copy of the Report of the Poor Law Commissioners Relative to Certain Charges which have been Disallowed by the Auditors of Unions in England and Wales, P.P., 1838, XXXVIII.

Fifth Annual Report of the Poor Law Commissioners, P.P., 1839, XX.

Return of Parishes and Unions to which Orders for the Appointment of Paid Officers to Collect Poor Rates have been Issued, P.P., 1839, XLIV.

Sixth Annual Report of the Poor Law Commissioners, P.P., 1840, XVII.

Report of the Poor Law Commissioners . . . on the Continuance of the Poor Law Commission, P.P., 1840, XVII.

Report of Robert Weale, Assistant Poor Law Commissioner, on the Comparative State of Pauperism in Agricultural and Manufacturing Unions, P.P., 1840, XXXIX.

Seventh Annual Report of the Poor Law Commissioners, P.P., 1841, XI.

Eighth Annual Report of the Poor Law Commissioners, P.P., 1842, XIX.

Return of the Average Annual Expenditure of the Parishes Comprised in Each Union in England and Wales . . . [and] Orders for Relief Out of the House Given Since the Passing of the [Poor Law Amendment] Act by Justices of the Peace, P.P., 1842, XXXV.

Report from the Select Committee on Labouring Poor (Allotments of Land), P.P., 1843, VII.

Ninth Annual Report of the Poor Law Commissioners, P.P., 1843, XXI.

Copy of Instructions to Assistant Commissioners to Inquire into the State of the Gilbert's Act Incorporations, . . . With the Reports of the Assistant Commissioners, P.P., 1843, XLV.

Report from the Select Committee on Poor Relief (Gilbert Unions), P.P., 1844, X.

Tenth Annual Report of the Poor Law Commissioners, P.P., 1844, XIX.

Return of the Number of Able-Bodied Persons and Their Families (Not Being Sick) by Whom Application for Relief has been Made . . . in the Counties of Dorset, Wilts, Berks, Oxford, Buckingham, and Bedford, P.P., 1844, XL.

Report from the Select Committee on Gilbert Unions, P.P., 1845, XIII.

Eleventh Annual Report of the Poor Law Commissioners, P.P., 1845, XXVII.

Twelfth Annual Report of the Poor Law Commissioners, P.P., 1846, XIX.

Return of the Total Population of Great Britain in 1831 and 1841, also of the Number of Adult Males Employed in Agriculture, P.P. (Lords), 1846, XIX.

First Report from the Select Committee on Settlement and Poor Removal, P.P., 1847, XI.

Thirteenth Annual Report of the Poor Law Commissioners, P.P., 1847, XXVIII.

Fourteenth Annual Report of the Poor Law Commissioners, P.P., 1847-8, XXXIII.

Returns of the Land Tax Quotas . . . and Return of Money Levied for Poor Rate and County Rate, P.P., 1849, XLVI.

Reports of the Poor Law Board on the Laws of Settlement and Removal of the Poor, P.P., 1850, XXVII.

Report of George Coode to the Poor Law Board on the Law of Settlement and Removal of the Poor, P.P., 1851, XXVI.

Reports to the Poor Law Board on the Operation of the Law of Settlement, on Rating, and on Close and Open Parishes, P.P. (Lords), 1851, XXXI.

A Return of the Number of Persons to Whom Voting Papers Were Delivered at the Last March Election of Guardians . . ., P.P. (Lords), 1852-3, IX.

Returns Relating to Contested Elections of Boards of Guardians, P.P., 1857, XXXII.

Reports of Poor Law Inspectors on the Boundaries of Poor Law Unions, 1870, LVIII.

Report from the Select Committee on Boundaries of Parishes, Unions, and Counties, P.P., 1873, VIII.

Report from the Select Committee on Poor Law Guardians, P.P., 1878, XVII.

Return of the Number of Chairmen and Vice-Chairmen of Boards of Guardians who are Ex-Officio Members or are Elected Guardians, P.P., 1893, LXXVII.

III. Books

Anon. The History of the Times. "The Thunderer" in the Making, 1785-1841. London: The Times, 1935.

Aschrott, P.F. The English Poor Law System, Past and Present. London: Knight and Co., 1902.

Ashby, A.W. One Hundred Years of Poor Law Administration in a Warwickshire Village. Oxford: Clarendon Press, 1912.

Aspinall, A. Lord Brougham and the Whig Party. Manchester: Manchester University Press, 1927.

Aspinall, A. (ed.). Three Early Nineteenth Century Diaries. London: Williams and Norgate Ltd., 1952.

Baxter, G.R.W. The Book of the Bastiles. London: John Stephens, 1841.

Beales, Hugh L. The Making of Social Policy. London: Oxford University Press, 1946.

Beloff, Max. Public Order and Popular Disturbances, 1660-1714. Oxford: University Press, 1938.

Black, Eugene C. (ed.). Victorian Culture and Society. New York: Walker and Company, 1974.

Board of Agriculture. The Agricultural State of the Kingdom. New York: Augustus M. Kelley, 1970 (First published 1816).

Bovill, E.W. English Country Life, 1780-1830. London: Oxford University Press, 1963.

Bowley, Marian. Nassau Senior and Classical Economics. London: George Allen & Unwin Ltd., 1937.

Brock, Michael. The Great Reform Act. London: Hutchinson & Co. Ltd., 1973.

Bruce, Maurice. The Coming of the Welfare State. London: B.J. Batsford Ltd., 1965.

Buchanan, A.C. Emigration Practically Considered. . . . London: Henry Colburn, 1828.

Burrow, J.W. Evolution and Society. Cambridge: University Press, 1970.

Caird, James. English Agriculture in 1850-51. London: Frank Cass and Co. Ltd., 1968 (2nd edition).

Caird, James. The Landed Interest and the Supply of Food. New York: Frank Cass & Co., 1967 (First published in 1878).

Carus-Wilson, E.M. (ed.). Essays in Economic History. London: Edward Arnold Ltd., 1962.

Chadwick, Edwin. Report on the Sanitary Condition of the Labouring Population of Great Britain, edited by M.W. Flinn. Edinburgh: University Press, 1965 (First published 1842).

Chambers, J.D. and G.E. Mingay. The Agricultural Revolution, 1750-1880. New York: Schocken Books, 1966.

Chambers, J.D. Nottinghamshire in the Eighteenth Century. A Study of Life and Labour Under the Squirearchy. New York: Augustus M. Kelley, 1966.

Clapham, J.H. An Economic History of Modern Britain: The Early Railway Age, 1820-1850. Cambridge: University Press, 1926.

Clarke, John J. Public Assistance. London: Sir Isaac Pitman and Sons Ltd., 1934.

Clokie, H.M. and J.W. Robinson. Royal Commissions of Inquiry. Stanford: Stanford University Press, 1937.

Coats, A.W. (ed.). Poverty in the Victorian Age. Farnborough: Gregg, 1973.

Cole, G.D.H. and A.W. Filson. British Working Class Movements. London: Macmillan and Co. Ltd., 1951.

Dalton, George. Economic Systems and Society. Harmondsworth: Penguin, 1974.

Darvall, F.O. Popular Disturbances and Public Order in Regency England. London: Humphrey Milford, 1934.

Davis, Richard W. Political Change and Continuity, 1760-1885: A Buckinghamshire Study. Newton Abbot, Devon: David & Charles, 1972.

De Ruggiero, Guido. The History of European Liberalism. Boston: Beacon Press, 1967.

Dicey, A.V. Lectures on the Relation Between Law and Public Opinion in England During the Nineteenth Century. London: Macmillan and Co., 1917 (2nd edition).

Driver, Cecil. Tory Radical. New York: Oxford University Press, 1946.

Dunbabin, J.P.D. Rural Discontent in Nineteenth-Century Britain. London: Faber and Faber, 1974.

Edsall, Nicholas C. The Anti-Poor Law Movement. New Jersey: Rowman & Littlefield Inc., 1971.

Ernle, Lord. English Farming Past and Present. Chicago: Quadrangle Books, 1961.

Fay, C.R. Life and Labour in the Nineteenth Century. Cambridge: University Press, 1920.

Finer, S.E. The Life and Times of Sir Edwin Chadwick. London: Methuen & Co. Ltd., 1952.

Fussell, G.E. From Tolpuddle to T.U.C.: A Century of Farm Labourers' Politics. Slough: The Windsor Press, 1948.

Fussell, G.E. Village Life in the Eighteenth Century. Worcester: Littlebury and Co., n.d.

Gash, Norman. Reaction and Reconstruction in English Politics, 1832-1852. Oxford: Clarendon Press, 1965.

Gash, Norman. Sir Robert Peel: The Life of Sir Robert Peel after 1830. London: Longmans, 1972.

Gill, J.C. The Ten Hours Parson. London: S.P.C.K., 1959.

Goffman, Ewing. Interaction Ritual. Chicago: Aldine Publishing Co., 1967.

Goldstrom, J.M. The Social Content of Education, 1808-1870. Shannon, Ireland: Irish University Press, 1972.

Grote, Mrs. George. The Philosophical Radicals of 1832. London: Savill and Edwards, 1866.

Halevy, Elie. The Growth of Philosophic Radicalism. Boston: Beacon Press, 1966.

Halevy, Elie. The Triumph of Reform, 1830-1841. London: Benn, 1950.

Hamburger, Joseph. Intellectuals in Politics: John Stuart Mill and the Philosophic Radicals. New Haven: Yale University Press, 1965.

Hammond, J.L. and Barbara. The Village Labourer, 1760-1832. London: Longmans, Green, and Co., 1912.

Hampson, E.M. The Treatment of Poverty in Cambridgeshire, 1597-1834. Cambridge: University Press, 1934.

Harrison, J.F.C. The Early Victorians, 1832-1851. New York: Praeger, 1971.

Hartwell, R.M. (ed.). The Industrial Revolution. New York: Barnes & Noble, 1970.

Hasbach, W. A History of the English Agricultural Labourer. London: P.S. King & Son, 1908.

Hobsbawm, E.J. and George Rudé. Captain Swing. New York: Pantheon Books, 1968.

Hobsbawm, E.J. Labouring Men. London: Weidenfeld and Nicolson, 1964.

Hodder, Edwin. The Life and Work of the Seventh Earl of Shaftesbury. London: Cassell & Co. Ltd., 1888.

Holyoake, G.J. Life of Joseph Raynor Stephens. London:

Williams and Norgate, 1881.

Hughes, Edward (ed.). The Diaries and Correspondence of James Losh, 1811-1833. Durham: Andrews & Co., 1963.

Inglis, Brian. Poverty and the Industrial Revolution. London: Hodder and Stoughton, 1971.

Jackson, J.A. (ed.). Social Stratification. Cambridge: University Press, 1968.

Johnston, H.J.M. British Emigration Policy, 1815-1830. Oxford: Clarendon Press, 1972.

Jones, E.L. and G.E. Mingay (eds.). Land, Labour and Population in the Industrial Revolution. New York: Barnes & Noble Inc., 1968.

Kitson Clark, G. Churchmen and the Condition of England, 1832-1885. London: Methuen & Co. Ltd., 1973.

Kitson Clark, G. The Making of Victorian England. Cambridge, Mass.: Harvard University Press, 1962.

Kitson Clark, G. Peel and the Conservative Party. London: Frank Cass & Co. Ltd., 1964.

Laslett, Peter. The World We Have Lost. New York: Charles Scribner's Sons, 1965.

Levy, S. Leon. Nassau W. Senior, 1790-1864. Newton Abbot, Devon: David & Charles, 1970.

Lewis, R.A. Edwin Chadwick and the Public Health Movement, 1832-1854. London: Longmans, Green and Co., 1952.

Lubenow, William C. The Politics of Government Growth. Early Victorian Attitudes Toward State Intervention, 1833-1848. Newton Abbot, Devon: David & Charles, 1971.

Lubove, Roy (ed.). Social Welfare in Transition, 1834-1909. Pittsburgh: Pittsburgh University Press, 1966.

Mackay, Thomas. A History of the English Poor Law, vol. III. London: P.S. King and Son, 1899.

Mackay, Thomas. Public Relief of the Poor. London: John Murray, 1901.

Mackenzie, W.J.M. and J.W. Grove. Central Administration in Britain. London: Longmans, Green and Co. Ltd., 1965.

Macpherson, C.B. The Political Theory of Possessive Individualism. Oxford: Oxford University Press, 1967.

Marshall, Dorothy. The English Poor in the Eighteenth Century. London: George Routledge and Sons Ltd., 1926.

Marshall, J.D. The Old Poor Law, 1795-1834. London: Macmillan, 1968.

Marston, Maurice. Sir Edwin Chadwick. London: Leonard Parsons Ltd., 1925.

Martin, E.W. (ed.). Comparative Development in Social Welfare. New York: George Allen & Unwin, 1972.

Mather, F.C. Public Order in the Age of the Chartists. Manchester: Manchester University Press, 1959.

Mathias, Peter. The First Industrial Nation. New York: Charles Scribner's Sons, 1969.

Midwinter, E.C. Social Administration in Lancashire, 1830-1860. Manchester: Manchester University Press, 1969.

Mill, J.S. Autobiography. Indianapolis: Liberal Arts Press Inc., 1957.

Mills, Dennis R. (ed.). English Rural Communities: The Impact of a Specialised Economy. London: Macmillan, 1973.

Mingay, G.E. Enclosure and the Small Farmer in the Age of the Industrial Revolution. London: Macmillan, 1968.

Mingay, G.E. English Landed Society in the Eighteenth Century. London: Routledge and Kegan Paul, 1963.

Morley, John. The Life of William Ewart Gladstone. London: Macmillan and Co. Ltd., 1903.

Nelson, R.R. The Home Office, 1782-1801. Durham, N.C.: Duke University Press, 1969.

Nicholls, Sir George. A History of the English Poor Law, vol. II. New York: G.P. Putnam's Sons, 1898.

Nisbet, Robert A. The Quest for Community. New York: Oxford University Press, 1953.

Nisbet, Robert A. The Social Bond. New York: Alfred A. Knopf, 1970.

Nisbet, Robert A. Tradition and Revolt: Historical and Sociological Essays. New York: Random House, 1970.

Owen, David. English Philanthropy, 1660-1960. Cambridge, Mass.: Harvard University Press, 1965.

Oxley, Geoffrey W. Poor Relief in England and Wales, 1601-1834. Newton Abbot, Devon: David & Charles, 1974.

Parker, Charles Stuart. Sir Robert Peel. London: John Murray, vol I: 1891, vols. II & III: 1899.

Parris, Henry. Constitutional Bureaucracy. London: George Allen & Unwin Ltd., 1969.

Peacock, A.J. Bread or Blood. A Study of the Agrarian Riots in East Anglia in 1816. London: Victor Gollanez Ltd., 1965.

Perkin, Harold. The Origins of Modern English Society, 1780-1880. Toronto: Toronto University Press, 1972.

Polanyi, Karl. The Great Transformation. New York: Farrar & Rinehart Inc., 1944.

Poynter, J.R. Society and Pauperism: English Ideas on Poor Relief, 1795-1834. London: Routledge & Kegan Paul, 1969.

Prest, John. Lord John Russell. London: Macmillan, 1972.

Ramsay, A.A.W. Sir Robert Peel. Freeport, New York: Books for Libraries Press, 1969.

Reaney, Bernard. The Class Struggle in 19th Century Oxfordshire. History Workshop Pamphlets, No. 3. Oxford: History Workshop, Ruskin College, n.d.

Redford, Arthur. Labour Migration in England, 1800-50. Manchester: Manchester University Press, 1926.

Redlich, J. and F.W. Hirst. Local Government in England. London: Macmillan and Co. Ltd., 1903.

Reeve, Henry (ed.). The Greville Memoirs: A Journal of the Reigns of King George IV and King William IV. London: Longmans, Green, and Co., 1875.

Robbins, Lionel. The Theory of Economic Policy in English Classical Political Economy. London: Macmillan & Co. Ltd., 1961.

Roberts, David. Victorian Origins of the British Welfare State. New Haven: Yale University Press, 1960.

Rose, M.E. (ed.). The English Poor Law, 1780-1930. Newton Abbot, Devon: David & Charles, 1971.

Rose, M.E. The Relief of Poverty, 1834-1914. London: Macmillan, 1972.

Roseveare, Henry. The Treasury: The Evolution of a British Institution. London: The Penguin Press, 1969.

Russell, Lord. Recollections and Suggestions, 1813-1873. London: Longmans, Green, and Co., 1875.

Russell, Rollo. Early Correspondence of Lord John Russell. London: T. Fisher Unwin, 1913.

Sanders, Lloyd C. (ed.). Lord Melbourne's Papers. New York: Kraus Reprint Co., 1971 (First published 1889).

Senior, N.W. A Letter to Lord Howick on a Legal Provision for the Irish Poor. London: John Murray, 1831.

Senior, N.W. Letters on the Factory Act. London: B. Fellowes, 1837.

Senior, N.W. Three Lectures on the Rate of Wages . . . [and] the Causes and Remedies of the Present Disturbances. London: John Murray, 1830.

Slater, Gilbert. Poverty and the State. London: Constable and Co. Ltd., 1930.

Smith, Frank. The Life and Work of Sir James Kay-Shuttleworth. London: John Murray, 1923.

Spring, David. The English Landed Estate in the Nineteenth Century: Its Administration. Baltimore: The Johns Hopkins Press, 1963.

Sutherland, Gillian (ed.). Studies in the Growth of

Nineteenth-Century Government. London: Routledge & Kegan Paul Ltd., 1972.

Tate, W.E. The English Village Community and the Enclosure Movement. London: Victor Gollanez Ltd., 1967.

Tate, W.E. The Parish Chest. Cambridge: University Press, 1960.

Taylor, Arthur J. Laissez-faire and State Intervention in Nineteenth-century Britain. London: Macmillan Press, 1972.

Thompson, E.P. The Making of the English Working Class. Hammondsworth, Middlesex: Penguin Books, 1968.

Thompson, E.P. Whigs and Hunters. The Origin of the Black Act. New York: Random House, 1975.

Thompson, F.M.L. English Landed Society in the Nineteenth Century. London: Routledge & Kegan Paul, 1963.

Thornton, A.P. The Habit of Authority. Paternalism in British History. Toronto: University of Toronto Press, 1966.

Vancouver, Charles. General View of the Agriculture of the County of Devon. New York: Augustus M. Kelley, 1969 (First published 1808).

Ward, J.T. (ed.). Popular Movements, 1830-1850. London: Macmillan & Co. Ltd., 1970.

Ward, J.T. Sir James Graham. London: St. Martin's Press, 1967.

Webb, Robert K. Harriet Martineau: A Radical Victorian. New York: Columbia University Press, 1960.

Webb, Sidney and Beatrice. English Poor Law History, Part I: The Old Poor Law. Hamden, Conn.: Archon Books, 1963.

Webb, Sidney and Beatrice. English Poor Law History, Part II: The Last Hundred Years. Hamden, Conn.: Archon Books, 1963.

Webb, Sidney and Beatrice. English Poor Law Policy. London: Frank Cass and Co. Ltd., 1963.

Williams, David. The Rebecca Riots. A Study in Agrarian Discontent. Cardiff: University of Wales Press, 1955.

Wilmot Horton, R. Causes and Remedies of Pauperism. Fourth Series. Explanation of Mr. Wilmot Horton's Bill, in a Letter and Queries Addressed to N.W. Senior, with his Answers. London: Edmund Lloyd, 1830.

Young, Arthur. General View of the Agriculture of the County of Norfolk. New York: Augustus M. Kelley, 1969 (First published 1804).

IV. Articles

Aldcroft, Derek H. "The 'Revolt of the Field'," Past and Present, 27 (1964), 109.

Arnold, Rollo. "The 'Revolt of the Field' in Kent 1872-1879," Past and Present, 64 (1974), 71-95.

Baugh, D.A. "The Cost of Poor Relief in South-East England, 1790-1834," Economic History Review, Second Series, XXVIII (1975), 61-77.

Beales, H.L. "The New Poor Law," History, XV (1931), 308-19.

Beier, A.L. "Vagrants and the Social Order in Elizabethan England," Past and Present, 64 (1974), 3-29.

Bell, Colin and Howard Newby. "The Sources of Variation in Agricultural Workers' Images of Society," The Sociological Review, XXI, 2 (1973), 229-53.

Blaug, Mark. "The Myth of the Old Poor Law and the Making of the New," Journal of Economic History, XXIII, 2 (1963), 151-84.

Blaug, Mark. "The Poor Law Report Reexamined," Journal of Economic History, XXIV, 2 (1964), 229-45.

Boyson, Rhodes. "The New Poor Law in North-East Lancashire, 1834-71," Transactions of the Lancashire and Cheshire Antiquarian Society, LXX (1960), 35-56.

Brebner, J. Bartlet. "Laissez Faire and State Intervention in Nineteenth-Century Britain," Journal of Economic History, Supplement VIII (1948), 59-73.

Brundage, Anthony. "The English Poor Law of 1834 and the Cohesion of Agricultural Society," Agricultural History, XLVIII, 3 (1974), 405-17.

Brundage, Anthony. "The Landed Interest and the New Poor Law: A Reappraisal of the Revolution in Government," English Historical Review, LXXXVIII, 342 (1972), 27-48.

Brundage, Anthony. "The Landed Interest and the New Poor Law: A Reply," English Historical Review, XC, 355 (1975), 347-51.

Brundage, Anthony. "The Origins of the New Poor Law: Some Lines of Inquiry," Albion, VI, 1 (1974), 76-77.

Chambers, J.D. "The Making of the English Working Class," History, LI (1966), 183-88.

Checkland, S.G. "The Propagation of Ricardian Economics in England," Economica, XVI, 61 (1949), 40-52.

Clapham, J.H. "The Growth of an Agrarian Proletariat, 1688-1832," Cambridge Historical Journal, I, 1 (1923), 92-95.

Coates, Willson H. "Benthamism, Laissez Faire, and Collectivism," Journal of the History of Ideas, II (1950), 357-63.

Coats, A.W. "Changing Attitudes to Labour in the Mid-Eighteenth Century," Economic History Review, Second Series, XI, 1 (1958), 35-51.

Coats, A.W. "Contrary Moralities: Plebs, Paternalists and Political Economists," Past and Present, 54 (1972), 130-33.

Coats, A.W. "Economic Thought and Poor Law Policy in the Eighteenth Century," Economic History Review, Second Series, XIII, 1 (1960), 39-51.

Collins, E.J.T. "Harvest Technology and Labour Supply in Britain," Economic History Review, Second Series, XXII, 3 (1969), 453-73.

Coleman, D.C. "Labour in the English Economy of the 17th Century," Economic History Review, Second Series, VIII, 3 (1956), 280-92.

Cowherd, Raymond G. "The Humanitarian Reform of the English Poor Laws from 1782 to 1815," Proceedings of the American Philosophical Society, CIV, 3 (1960), 328-42.

Cromwell, Valerie. "Interpretations of Nineteenth-Century Administration: An Analysis," Victorian Studies, IX, 3 (1966), 245-55.

Crough, R.L. "Laissez-Faire in Nineteenth Century Britain: Myth or Reality," Manchester School of Economic and Social Studies, XXXV, 3 (1967), 199-215.

Duke, Francis. "The Poor Law Commissioners and Education," Journal of Educational Administration and History, III, 1 (1970), 7-13.

Dunbabin, J.P.D. "The 'Revolt of the Field': The Agricultural Labourers' Movement in the 1870s," Past and Present, 26 (1963), 68-97.

Flinn, M.W. "The Poor Employment Act of 1817," Economic History Review, Second Series, XIV, 1 (1961), 82-92.

Fraser, Peter. "Public Petitioning and Parliament before 1832," History, XLVI, 158 (1961), 195-211.

Gash, Norman. "Rural Unemployment, 1815-34," Economic History Review, VI (1935-6), 90-93.

Gutchen, Robert M. "Local Improvements and Centralization in Nineteenth-Century England," Historical Journal, IV, 1 (1961), 85-96.

Harrison, J.F.C. "A Knife and Fork Question? Some Recent Writings on the History of Social Movements," Victorian Studies, XVIII, 2 (1974), 219-24.

Hart, J. "Nineteenth-Century Social Reform: A Tory Interpretation of History," Past and Present, 31 (1965), 39-61.

Healy, M.J.R. and E.L. Jones. "Wheat Yields in England, 1815-59," Journal of the Royal Statistical Society, 125, Part 4 (1962), 574-79.

Hennock, E.P. "The Sociological Premises of the First Reform Act: A Critical Note," Victorian Studies, XIV, 3 (1971), 321-27.

Henriques, U.R.Q. "Bastardy and the New Poor Law," Past and Present, 37 (1967), 103-29.

Henriques, U.R.Q. "How Cruel Was the Victorian Poor

Law?," Historical Journal, XI, 2 (1968), 365-71.

Himmelfarb, Gertrude. "The Writing of Social History: Recent Studies in Nineteenth-Century England," Journal of British Studies, XI, 1 (1971), 148-69.

Hobsbawm, E.J. "From Social History to the History of Society," Daedalus, C, 1 (1971), 20-45.

Holderness, B.A. "'Open' and 'Close' Parishes in England in the Eighteenth and Nineteenth Centuries," Agricultural History Review, XX (1972), 126-39.

Hume, L.J. "Jeremy Bentham and the Nineteenth-Century Revolution in Government," Historical Journal, X, 4 (1967), 361-75.

Hume, L.J. "Myrdal on Jeremy Bentham: Laissez Faire and Harmony of Interests," Economica, XXXVI, 143 (1969), 295-303.

Hunt, H.G. "Landownership and Enclosure, 1750-1830," Economic History Review, Second Series, XI, 3 (1959), 497-505.

Hutchison, T.W. "Bentham as an Economist," The Economic Journal, LXVI (1956), 288-306.

Huzel, James P. "Malthus, the Poor Law, and Population in Early Nineteenth-Century England," Economic History Review, Second Series, XXII, 3 (1969), 430-52.

Jones, E.L. "The Agricultural Labour Market in England, 1793-1872," Economic History Review, Second Series, XVII, 2 (1964), 322-38.

Jones, E.L. "English Farming before and during the Nineteenth Century," Economic History Review, Second Series, XV, 1 (1962), 145-52.

Kitson Clark, G. "The Repeal of the Corn Laws and the

Politics of the Forties," Economic History Review, Second Series, IV, 1 (1951), 1-13.

Kitson Clark, G. "Statesmen in Disguise: Reflexions on the History of the Neutrality of the Civil Service," Historical Journal, II, 1 (1959), 19-39.

Krause, J.T. "Changes in English Fertility and Mortality, 1781-1850," Economic History Review, Second Series, XI, 1 (1958), 52-70.

Lewis, R.A. "William Day and the Poor Law Commissioners," University of Birmingham Historical Journal, IX (1964), 163-96.

MacDonagh, O. "The Nineteenth-Century Revolution in Government: A Reappraisal," Historical Journal, I, 1 (1958), 52-67.

MacLeod, Roy M. "Statesmen Undisguised," American Historical Review, LXXVIII, 5 (1973), 1386-1405.

Marshall, J.D. "The Nottinghamshire Reformers and Their Contribution to the New Poor Law," Economic History Review, Second Series, XIII, 3 (1961), 382-96.

Mather, F.C. "The Railways, the Electric Telegraph and Public Order During the Chartist Period, 1837-48," History, XXXVIII (1953), 40-53.

McCord, Norman. "The Implementation of the 1834 Poor Law Amendment Act on Tyneside," International Review of Social History, XIV (1969), 90-108.

McCord, Norman. "The Government of Tyneside, 1800-1850," Transactions of the Royal Historical Society, XX (1970), 5-30.

Midwinter, E.C. "State Intervention at the Local Level: The New Poor Law in Lancashire," Historical Journal, X, 1 (1967), 106-12.

Moore, D.C. "Concession or Cure: the Sociological Premises of the First Reform Act," Historical Journal, IX, 1 (1966), 39-59.

Moore, D.C. "The Other Face of Reform," Victorian Studies, V, 1 (1961), 7-34.

Neuman, Mark D. "A Suggestion Regarding the Origins of the Speenhamland Plan," English Historical Review, LXXXIV, 331 (1969), 317-22.

Newby, Howard. "The Deferential Dialectic," Comparative Studies in Society and History, XVII, 2 (1975), 139-64.

Oldham, C.R. "Oxfordshire Poor Law Papers," Economic History Review, V, 1 (1934-5), 87-97.

Parris, Henry. "The Nineteenth-Century Revolution in Government: A Reappraisal Reappraised," Historical Journal, III, 1 (1960), 17-37.

Plowman, D.E.G. and W.E. Minchinton and Margaret Stacey. "Local Social Status in England and Wales," The Sociological Review, X, 2 (1962), 161-202.

Richards, Eric. "'Captain Swing' in the West Midlands," International Review of Social History, XIX (1974), Pt. 1, 86-99.

Roberts, David. "How Cruel Was the Victorian Poor Law?," Historical Journal, VI, 1 (1963), 97-107.

Roberts, David. "Jeremy Bentham and the Victorian Administrative State," Victorian Studies, II (1959), 193-210.

Rose, M.E. "The Allowance System Under the New Poor Law," Economic History Review, Second Series, XIX, 3 (1966), 607-20.

Rose, M.E. "The Anti-Poor Law Movement in the North

of England," Northern History, I (1966), 70-91.

Rose, R.B. "Eighteenth Century Price Riots and Public Policy in England," International Review of Social History, VI (1961), 277-92.

Rudé, G. "English Rural and Urban Disturbances on the Eve of the First Reform Bill, 1830-1831," Past and Present, 37 (1967), 87-102.

Russell, Lord John. "The Improvement of the Law, Education, Health, and Morals of the People," pamphlet of The National Association for the Promotion of Social Science. Liverpool: Benson & Mallett, 1858.

Spring, David. "Lord Chandos and the Farmers, 1818-1846," Huntington Library Quarterly, XXXIII, 3 (1970), 257-81.

Spring, David. "The Role of the Aristocracy in the Late Nineteenth Century," Victorian Studies, IV, 1 (1960), 55-64.

Stacey, Margaret. "The Myth of Community Studies," British Journal of Sociology, XX, 2 (1969), 134-47.

Sutherland, Gillian. "Recent Trends in Administrative History," Victorian Studies, XIII, 4 (1970), 408-11.

Swart, K.W. "'Individualism' in the Mid-Nineteenth Century (1826-1860)," Journal of the History of Ideas, XXIII (1962), 77-90.

Taylor, James Stephen. "The Mythology of the Old Poor Law," Journal of Economic History, XXIX, 2 (1969), 292-97.

Thompson, E.P. "The Moral Economy of the English Crowd in the Eighteenth Century," Past and Present,

50 (1971), 76-136.

Thompson, E.P. "Patrician Society, Plebian Culture," Journal of Social History, VII, 4 (1974), 382-405.

Thompson, F.M.L. "The Social Distribution of Landed Property in England since the Sixteenth Century," Economic History Review, Second Series, XIX, 3 (1966), 505-17.

Thompson, F.M.L. "Whigs and Liberals in the West Riding, 1830-1860," English Historical Review, CCXCI (1959), 214-39.

Tyrell, A. "Political Economy, Whiggism and the Education of Working-Class Adults in Scotland, 1817-40," Scottish Historical Review, XLIX (1969), 151-65.

Viner, Jacob. "Adam Smith and Laissez Faire," Journal of Political Economy, XXV, 2 (1927), 198-232.

Viner, Jacob. "Bentham and J.S. Mill: The Utilitarian Background," American Economic Review, XXXIX, 2 (1949), 360-82.

Willson, F.M. "Ministries and Boards: Some Aspects of Administrative Development Since 1832," Public Administration, XXXIII (1955), 43-58.

Zangerl, C.H.E. "The Social Composition of the County Magistracy in England and Wales, 1831-1887," Journal of British Studies, XI, 1 (1971), 113-25.

INDEX